Thomas I. White

Upsala College

Right and Wrong

a brief guide to understanding ethics

PRENTICE HALL, Englewood Cliffs, New Jersey 07632

Library of Congress Cataloging-in-Publication Data

WHITE, THOMAS I.
  Right and wrong.

  Bibliography: p.
  Includes index.
  1. Ethics. I. Title.
  BJ1012.W5   1988   170   87–19369
  ISBN 0–13–781170–5

Editorial/production supervision: Linda B. Pawelchak
Cover design: Lundgren Graphics, Ltd
Manufacturing buyer: Margaret Rizzi

To Daisy—who opened the door.

© 1988 by Prentice Hall
A Division of Simon & Schuster
Englewood Cliffs, New Jersey 07632

Printed in the United States of America

10 9 8 7 6 5 4 3 2 1

ISBN 0-13-781170-5 01

Prentice-Hall International (UK) Limited, *London*
Prentice-Hall of Australia Pty. Limited, *Sydney*
Prentice-Hall Canada Inc., *Toronto*
Prentice-Hall Hispanoamericana, S.A., *Mexico*
Prentice-Hall of India Private Limited, *New Delhi*
Prentice-Hall of Japan, Inc., *Tokyo*
Simon & Schuster Asia Pte. Ltd., *Singapore*
Editora Prentice-Hall do Brasil, Ltda., *Rio de Janeiro*

Contents

2

An "Ethical Yardstick"   19

3

Measuring Consequences   39

Preface

Somewhere over the last quarter century, America lost its "moral rudder." We have gone from a nation committed to moral idealism to being reluctant spectators of one scandal after another. We have seen so much wrongdoing in government, business, education, and even religion, that unethical behavior has simply become "business as usual" in some quarters of the society. And what's the most telling sign of how bad it's become? We aren't even shocked anymore.

The current state of affairs, however, should come as no surprise to any of us. Over the last twenty years, the actions of many of our most prominent leaders in business and government have encouraged the rest of us—and especially the young—to follow their examples of selfishness and acquisitiveness. Too many of our leading citizens have secured their own interest at the expense of others around them. In defiance of this nation's most prized values, they regularly compromise the public good to advance their own fortunes, or the success of their companies or ideologies. Consequently, idealism has given way to cynicism, altruism to self-interest, charity to greed, and kindness to meanness.

Despite the variety of wrongdoing we've witnessed, the basic elements are the same. Otherwise intelligent, capable, and responsible people have been either morally blind or totally contemptuous of the fact that what they're doing is wrong. The conclusion we're led to is as clear as it is troubling—the spirit of America at the end of the twentieth century is captured less by "With liberty and justice for all" and "Give me your tired, your poor" than by "Looking out for Number One," "What's right is what's right for *me*," and "Everybody else is doing it, why shouldn't I?"

Fortunately, there are signs that people in this country are now demanding that ethics be taken seriously again. Wrongdoing that used to be tolerated now evokes moral outrage and criminal indictments. Professional schools are introducing courses on ethics. And applied ethics is being taken more seriously by the American philosophical "establishment." As a society we have realized that the cult of selfishness only undermines everything it touches.

This book aims to be part of the current resurgence of interest in ethics. My hope is that I have explained a philosophical approach to ethics in a more accessible and commonsense fashion than is usually the case with philosophy books, that I will help this book's readers in the difficult task of making their way through the ethical dilemmas that we all inevitably face, and that I have offered a persuasive argument for why the moral life is important. This book begins by discussing what philosophical ethics is and isn't (Chapter 1), moves on to describe a secular standard of right and wrong (Chapter 2), explains teleological and deontological approaches to ethics (Chapters 3 and 4), provides a rationale for ethical behavior (Chapter 5), and concludes with an extended analysis of an ethical dilemma (Chapter 6). The outlook and approach embodied in these pages are the result of more than fifteen years of teaching ethics.

These pages also contain much that I owe to other people—indeed more than I can acknowledge in a few words. My primary debt is to the nearly 400 students who endured earlier drafts of this book in my business ethics classes at Upsala College over the last three years. Their comments, reactions (and, sometimes, lack thereof) were of immense help. I would also like to thank Richard C. Conrath (Montcalm Community College), David B. Fletcher (Wheaton College), and Matthias T. Schulte (Montgomery College) who made a number of valuable suggestions. Of course, I accept full responsibility for whatever problems still remain. Finally, I would like to express my deep appreciation for the love, support, and encouragement of a number of special people I am fortunate to know. They make the world a gentler place for all who come in contact with them and they provide me with shelter from the storm.

Thomas I. White
Glen Ridge, New Jersey

Introduction

Imagine this scenario: One day your teacher comes into class and announces a major examination for the next day, thereby breaking a promise to give you two weeks' warning for any exam. What's your reaction? Or suppose you find out that your roommate has been "borrowing" money from your wallet without asking? Or what if someone stole a term paper you just finished and turned it in under his or her name?

You may react to these incidents with anything from anger to outrage. You may accuse your teacher of being "unfair" or use a few other choice words. You might forgive your friend, but you'd be upset by what he or she did. And you'd probably want the paper-thief drawn and quartered in front of the administration building.

On the other hand, think about what your reaction might be if your teacher cancelled the exam because someone reminded him of his promise. Or how would you feel if a friend went out of her way to help you out of a tight spot? You'd probably say your teacher had acted properly in keeping his word and that your friend had done a good deed. No doubt you'd think these people acted in some positive way, and that these actions were better than those depicted in the first situation.

Most of us evaluate people's actions all the time. Maybe it's on a vital issue like theft or heroism. Or perhaps it's a small favor or a broken date. We naturally measure the way people around us act.

This short guide will help you learn how to judge the morality of actions in a more sophisticated, rigorous, and clear-headed way. Specifically, it's an essay about **ethics.** We're going to look at how we evaluate whether actions are *right* or *wrong.* Ethics is about *evaluating actions.* When we do ethics, we make judgments about how right or wrong our own and other people's actions are.

Chapter 1 will begin with a general discussion about ethics—what it is, how it's done. We'll move on to develop what we might call an **ethical yardstick**—a basic standard we can use in evaluating actions (Chapter 2). We'll then take a careful look at a couple of ways we can use this yardstick in practice (Chapters 3, "Measuring Consequences," and 4, "Measuring Actions"). Next we'll talk about why we should bother to worry about the morality of what we do (Chapter 5, "Doing Right—Why Bother?"). And we'll end by applying all of this to a moral dilemma (Chapter 6, "Cheating: An Ethical Dilemma").

With patience, you'll learn a new way of measuring what people do. In fact, the goal is to introduce you to a world that's invisible and intangible and show you that you can weigh, measure, juggle, and manipulate intangibles as easily as if they were chairs and tables.

chapter 1

Ethics: What It Is, Does, and Isn't

PHILOSOPHICAL ETHICS

Let me begin with two propositions you'll probably reject: (1) ethics is something totally new to you, and (2) the ideas you currently have are really a mass of confusion.

Although ideas of right and wrong have been part of your life since infancy, you are probably unfamiliar with **philosophical ethics.** Parents, teachers, preachers, friends, and associates try to shape our conduct and beliefs, but most of them don't use a philosophical approach. They cajole, coddle, argue, encourage, bribe, and sometimes even threaten us into accepting their ideas or toeing the line. They may try to reason with us, but perhaps not very well. Intense and disciplined thinking about right and wrong is "something totally new to you."

You may not see it that way—you probably have deeply held beliefs about right and wrong, and assume that everyone's entitled to his or her own ideas. And you probably think that's all that ethics is about. Ethics *is* about right and wrong, but your ideas about ethics may still be a "mass of confusion."

With ethics, this "mass of confusion" is the conglomeration of beliefs, feelings, traditions, and ideas we're saddled with from childhood. Many of our beliefs are emotional—we believe something is wrong because we feel guilty when we do it. Others are practical—we get in trouble with the law or some other authority if we get caught. Still others depend on

6

pleasing other people—we follow the beliefs of our parents because we want their approval, or we go along with what our friends do so they'll continue to like us.

Those ideas about ethics are probably also contradictory. We may say or think one thing, but do another: "Stealing is wrong. But skipping out of a restaurant without paying the check isn't stealing. It's fun." Perhaps we have one set of rules for ourselves and another set for others: "It's O.K. for me to cheat on my girlfriend, but it'd be wrong if she saw some other guy." Maybe we believe what our religion says about right and wrong—we know we should feel guilty after doing something wrong. But we also know that we can feel really good after getting away with some pretty serious "sinning."

At this point in your life, you may not have a consistent set of values, or know why you believe what you do. And you might not be able to explain very convincingly what you mean by right and wrong.

The aim of this book is to make a philosopher out of you—someone who can slog through the confusion, put it in order, think about it clearly, understand why you believe what you do, and explain your beliefs to others. All it takes is patience and practice.

ETHICS: WHAT IS IT?

The simplest way to explain what ethics does is to say that it *evaluates human actions.* But obviously, ethics isn't the only enterprise that evaluates behavior. Law divides actions into "legal" and "illegal" and tells us that if we disobey we'll go to jail, pay a fine, or lose some privilege. Religions advise us what to believe and how to act if we want to please God, achieve eternal happiness, or avoid the fires of Hell. Psychiatry explains the difference between behavior that's "normal," "neurotic," and "psychotic." Medicine gives us a yardstick for deciding how "healthy" our behavior is—business, how "profitable."

But with so many different ways of measuring human behavior, how is ethics different? What is ethics? Does it have anything special to contribute apart from law and religion?

Ethics

Ethics (or moral philosophy) is a branch of philosophy that dates back two thousand years to Socrates, the ancient Greek philosopher who spent his days in the Athenian marketplace challenging people to think about how they lived. Socrates believed that his mission was to ask his fellow citizens, "Are you not ashamed of your eagerness to possess as much wealth, reputation, and honors as possible, while you do not care for nor give thought to wisdom and truth, or the best possible state of your soul?" Believing that "the most important thing is not life, but the good life," Socrates died rather than use unscrupulous ways to avoid being executed on trumped-up charges.

Socrates investigated human behavior, and that's what ethics does. But as we can see from the original meanings of "ethical" and "moral," this includes both *what* people do and *how* they do it.

"Ethics" and "morals" come to us from two words in ancient Greek and Latin, *ethos* and *mores;* both mean "character."* When we ask if an action is ethical, we can think, "Is it the sort of thing somebody with a 'good character' would do?" And when we say that Alex has a good character, we mean that we trust her to do the right thing—to keep her promises or be kind. But we're also saying something about the *way* she does things. Alex keeps her word because it's the right thing to do, not because she wants to impress people. She gives to charity out of generosity, not because it's a tax deduction. We're unimpressed if George keeps his promise only with people bigger than he is or if Dorothy is helpful only when there's an audience around. Acting "ethically" is connected with *what* a person is doing and *how* he or she is doing it.

Although the common aim of ethics is to evaluate what we do, people label actions when making ethical judgments. The most common are "right," "wrong," "good," and "bad." Sometimes we hear "moral" and "immoral," "ethical" and "unethical," "morally justifiable" and "morally unjustifiable." Other times people refer to particular virtues and talk about "just" and "unjust," "fair" and "unfair." Some people choose a more religious language and talk about "righteous" and "sinful," "good" and "evil," and "sacred" and "profane." No matter how we refer to it, we usually just start with a basic distinction between *positive* and *negative*.

In some areas, it's easy to distinguish between acceptable and unacceptable behavior. You can separate "legal" from "illegal" by looking at law books. If you work for a company which allows a certain number of sick days, reviewing the policy manual will tell you how much time you can take off before you get in trouble.

But what kind of a judgment are we offering when we say that an action is acceptable or unacceptable from an *ethical* viewpoint? This is the basic question in ethics. And because it's so important, the next chapter is devoted to it. Right now we'll look at what ethics *is*—its connection with philosophy—and then move on to what it *isn't*. In Chapter 2 we'll look at what goes on when we evaluate the ethical character of an

---

*Throughout this handbook, "ethical" and "moral" will be used interchangeably, although some authors distinguish between them. Both words are associated with right and wrong, so don't get confused with alternating between the two.

action, that is, when we make some judgment about how right or wrong an action is.

Ethics and Philosophy

Ethics is a part of philosophy. And like any part of philosophy, ethics uses *reason, logic, concepts* and *philosophical explanations* to analyze its problems and find its answers. Philosophical questions are abstract or conceptual, so the most important tool to use is your mind.

Philosophical problems don't arise because you lack empirical data, so they aren't going to be solved by digging up facts. The facts of a case certainly count in ethics, but assembling the empirical data is only a preliminary step. If you want to convince someone that your teacher was "unfair" in scheduling a surprise exam, the facts aren't as important as what you mean by "fair" and "unfair," and how the facts fit your understanding of those concepts. The facts ([1] at the start of the term your teacher said he'd give you two weeks' warning; [2] now he's giving you one day's notice) show that your teacher was "unfair" only if your notion of fairness means something like "keeping your word."

Similarly, what laws, sacred writings, or religious authorities say is not the final word in a strictly ethical investigation. Some illegal actions are quite ethical (breaking the speed limit while rushing a sick friend to the hospital) and many immoral actions are perfectly legal (misleading someone about how you feel just to seduce him or her). The Pope's judgment about abortion may settle the issue for Roman Catholics, but it doesn't make it wrong for members of other religions.

So more important than facts, laws, or precepts is what you do with them. Whenever you do ethics, you analyze actions and their consequences. You examine the relevant ethical concepts and see how they apply to the case. And when you come to some conclusion, you use your mind to craft an explanation or argument that lays out your analysis and explains your point of view. In ethics, what counts most is *what you think.*

There are two ways to understand the last sentence: "What counts most is what you *think*" and "What counts most is what *you* think." Each emphasis tells us a lot about what ethics *isn't.*

WHAT ETHICS ISN'T

Ethics and Emotion— "What Counts Most Is What You *Think*"

The first way to look at this sentence is, "What counts most is what you *think*." Not what you *feel*, but what you *think*. Many people have gotten into the habit of using the two as though they mean the same thing, saying both "I feel happy" and "I feel that stealing is wrong." But there's a big difference between thinking and feeling, and it's especially important to keep this straight.

Simply put, *feeling* statements describe our own internal, private, emotional, or physical states: "I feel happy," "I feel angry," "I feel depressed," "I feel like I'm in love," "I feel hot," "I feel cold." If you tell me that you feel unhappy or warm, I must accept that as your description of what it feels like from the inside. I can't debate it. It would be ridiculous for me to say, "No, you don't feel unhappy" or "You shouldn't feel unhappy." For whatever reasons, you do feel unhappy and that's all there is to it. If I care about you I might ask "Why do you feel unhappy?" Maybe there's something I can do to cheer you up or perhaps talking about your unhappiness would make you feel a little better. But I'm not asking you to justify your unhappiness to me, or defend why you're entitled to feel that way. Your feelings legitimately exist in and of themselves, and that's all that matters.

We really shouldn't use *feeling* statements to express our ethical convictions, then. Strictly speaking, if I say, "I *feel* that capital punishment is morally wrong," I'm saying that something about capital punishment makes me uneasy, unhappy, or distressed. What I should say instead is "Capital punishment makes me feel upset." But, of course, that kind of statement doesn't explain my moral evaluation of capital punishment very well. So if we want to say something's "wrong," we must change our language. We've got to use *thinking* statements.

Thinking statements are very different than *feeling* statements. They communicate an opinion we hold for specific *reasons*—reasons that we should be willing to make public. If someone says to you, "I think it's wrong if a man hires a pretty, young girl as his secretary instead of a more experienced but less attractive older woman," you're entitled to ask "Why?" and get an explanation.

Since the main tools of philosophical ethics are reason, logic, and arguments, we're going to depend more on thinking than feeling. When you analyze an ethical problem, use your mind—not your heart. Be prepared to give reasons for your position, listen to someone who disagrees with you, consider the merits of what they say, and have an intelligent response.

Keep in mind that philosophical ethics is a public enterprise. We're all expected to state publicly the reasons for what we believe so that other people can scrutinize our arguments and either be convinced by us or show us our mistakes. It's like a scientist who runs an experiment. She publicly reports her findings so that her colleagues can either confirm this work or refute her. Inquiries after truth have to be public so that people can talk about what's going on.

If I want to convince you that cheating on a test is morally wrong, I can't say just that it makes me upset when people cheat and leave it at that. If you hold the opposite view, there's no reason why my belief would make you change your mind. I must give you reasons that you find relevant and convincing. If both of us make our reasons public, we can scrutinize each other's evidence, and perhaps come to an agreement. But even if we continue to disagree, we'll at least understand each other better and not think that our respective positions are arbitrary, self-serving, or baseless—unless that's what our explanations reveal!

There are, after all, better and worse reasons for holding certain positions, and this is precisely what ethics reveals. If I argue against cheating by pointing out that you would be gaining an unfair advantage over other students, I would be giving you an explanation worth considering. But if I say cheating is wrong because it lets too many students get high grades, I haven't given a reason for *why* it's wrong. My position, then, wouldn't be worthy of your respect. But going public with our explanations is the only way we'll find out.

The biggest problem with feeling statements is that we can't really argue with them. Feelings just have to be accepted. And if we can't argue about them, they won't get us very far in ethics. That's why, "What counts most is what you *think*."

Remember that people's emotions can change dramatically. On Monday we're in love with someone, on Tuesday we can't stand them, and on Wednesday we're back together. The first time we lie, we feel terribly guilty; the fifth time the guilt isn't so bad; and by the twentieth time we congratulate ourselves on how well we do it. How people feel about an action, particularly whether they feel guilty or not, doesn't really contribute much to an ethical investigation.

We should also not be misled by how sincerely people hold their beliefs. In the early years of this country, some people thought it was a good thing to burn "witches." Adolph Hitler sincerely believed that he was doing the world a favor by exterminating the Jews. More recently, terrorists who kill innocent people sincerely believe that they're doing the right thing. Sincerity is a wonderful human virtue, but is has absolutely nothing to do with being right.

This is not to say that human emotions are less important than reason or that they have no place in our lives. Feelings give color to our lives. And in some parts of life, like friendships and intimate relationships, we should pay more attention to our emotions than to our rational ideas.

Emotions can even be relevant to an ethical analysis. If you feel that lying is wrong, examining your feelings may reveal some of your reasons. Your feelings may be based on specific points of objection—like your concern that the person lied to is being manipulated. Or emotions may be important in ethics in a different way. Let's say we're weighing two murder cases. In one of them, the killer is a hit man who calmly and professionally killed a major politician. In the other, a woman who is continually beaten by her husband kills him in a rage. The difference in the emotional states of these two people is surely significant, and you may hold the woman less responsible for what she did. People's emotions affect why and how they do certain things. And this is relevant to analyzing and evaluating human behavior.

But we shouldn't put a lot of weight on how we react emotionally when deciding how morally acceptable an action is because our feelings will only cloud the issue, and we'll never get to the heart of the matter. A classic case of this is the way the abortion issue is being handled. Abortion's foes use sensationalistic films and photos of fetuses; its champions make stirring appeals to individual liberty and raise the grim specter of government regulation of our private lives. But so much emotion is stirred up that no one bothers to talk seriously abut the central questions: What does it take for something to be a person? And does a fetus meet those criteria?

So remember: In ethics, what counts most is what you *think*.

Ethics and Authority— "What Counts Most Is What *You* Think"

Now let's talk about the other way that sentence can be read. One of the most important characteristics of philosophy is that it grants total authority to us as rational individuals. In a philosophical discussion—one based on reason, logic, and argument—no special authority is granted to anyone or anything. A point is legitimate only if we agree that it is.

Imagine that I tell a friend that it's O.K. to discriminate against illegal aliens—to pay them poor wages and work them long hours under bad conditions. It doesn't matter if Socrates himself miraculously appears and tells me that what I'm advocating is wrong. We should not grant his point unless he convinces us with a decent explanation. He would give us his reasons, solicit our objections, consider and answer them. And this process would go on until we came to some agreement. The whole process works on discussion, disagreement, debate, and the free assent of individuals. As I said, what counts most is what *you* think, not what some authority tells you to think.

Obviously, not all discussions are conducted with this kind of openness to disagreement and dissent. When some people are faced with a dilemma about how they themselves or someone close to them should act, they decide on the basis of how things have always been done. They appeal to the authority of tradition ("We've done it this way in my family for generations, and we're going to continue."). Other people, notably parents, may simply appropriate a personal authority ("I'm your father and as long as you live under my roof, my word is law."). Still others will cite religious teachings ("The Bible teaches that adultery is a serious sin.").

What is common to all of these situations is that people are asking you to accept some *authority* as the final word on the matter. They are not trying to convince you or elicit your free consent that their position is correct. Appeals to authority are often accompanied by promises of rewards if you go along (your friends' approval, your parents' continued love) or threats of punishment if you disobey (ranging from being thrown out of the house to spending eternity being flame broiled). And as far as the authority is concerned, that's all there is to it.

I'm not saying that traditions, parental authority, and religions are foolish and meaningless. However, if we don't reason with each other, and instead try to manipulate by holding out rewards or threatening retaliation, we hardly treat one another with respect. Also, when you put together two groups of people who are absolutely sure they're right but hold opposite positions, you have a tinderbox. Both groups will have a low frustration threshold, and this makes for an explosive, potentially violent situation. As we read time and again in the pages of human history, when people get tired of using words against each other, and yet are still convinced they're right, they don't leave each other alone. They reach for weapons instead.

In any event, appeals to authority, threats, or coercion have no place in philosophical ethics. There is never a time in an ethical disagreement with someone when we can throw up our hands in disgust, yelling that further talk is useless, and stomp away cursing that anyone who disagrees with us is just going to have to give in—or else! One of the great strengths of philosophical ethics is that there are always good reasons to keep talking. You might think of a new argument that will finally convince your adversary. You could be persuaded by her that you've been wrong all along. Or you may find some new common ground.

Ethics and the Individual

Having said that "What counts most is what *you* think," I want to offer a caveat. I'm not saying that everyone is his or her own sole and ultimate authority on ethical questions. Philosophical ethics doesn't amount to the attitude that: "All morality is subjective and relative to the individual. If I think something is right for me, that makes it right." The authority of the individual goes only so far here.

The biggest problem with this thinking is that it violates obvious ideas of equality. It elevates you above all the people around you. It lets you say that if something is good for you, then nobody else's interests count. And such a presumption of personal superiority and authority doesn't fit with a rational, philosophical approach. What happens to discussion, debate, and mutual agreement with this attitude?

The other problem with this approach is that it simply isn't rationally defensible. As soon as you place sole moral authority with the individual, you open the door for some terrible things. If you say, "What's right depends on what the individual believes is right," you have absolutely no basis on which to condemn the actions of someone like Hitler. If a terrorist really believes that killing innocent people is right, how can you say that he's doing something wrong? If it all depends on the individual, why should your opinion count for more than his? Obviously, any system of ethics that can't condemn Hitler or terrorism leaves an enormous amount to be desired.

For all practical purposes, making the individual the ultimate moral authority reduces ethical disagreements to something akin to disputes about taste, likes, or dislikes. You may have heard the Latin expression, *De gustibus non est disputandum*—There's no arguing about taste. If someone's taste is different from yours, you simply have to accept it. Arguing won't change it because taste isn't a rational, intellectual matter. There are major problems, then, in giving the individual absolute and final authority in ethics.

Ethics and the Law

A different authority that some people appeal to in discussions about ethics is the law. Many people think that something is "wrong" only if the law prohibits it; conversely, if the law allows it, it's all right. However, we must reject this attitude because "legal" and "moral" are two different things.

A good illustration of the difference between "legal" and "moral" is in the classic western movie, *The Magnificent Seven*. The story revolves around the plight of a small Mexican village terrorized by a bandit. He and his gang regularly steal the crops and kill anyone who resists them. To protect themselves, the villagers hire seven gunfighters. After the first gun battle, however, one of the seven (Vin) wonders whether they've taken on more than they can handle, and another suggests that they leave, abandoning the villagers to the bandit. The group's leader (Chris) reminds them all that they made an agreement with the villagers. Vin points out that it's not a contract that a court of law would enforce. But Chris replies that doesn't matter—they still have to stick by their word. The responsibility Chris feels is clearly "moral" not "legal."

There's good reason why people confuse "legal" and "moral." Law gives us a yardstick to measure our actions against and it punishes people whose behavior falls short. And law does punish many actions that are morally wrong: murder, rape, theft, blackmail.

But there are problems with making the law an ultimate standard of right and wrong. The law allows many actions that are morally offensive (manipulating people or lying to your friends). It prohibits things that might be morally neutral or even good (certain sexual practices). And it is changeable and contradictory.

For nearly two centuries the laws of this country allowed atrocities to be done to black Americans. The laws first let them be owned, used, and abused as property. Even after emancipation the laws still allowed discrimination. The South African system of apartheid is built on legal foundations. And the ritual denial of fundamental human freedoms to the citizens of the Soviet Union is performed in accordance with its law codes.

Furthermore, when laws change, what was permitted on Monday can be punishable on Tuesday. Abortion used to be illegal; now it's allowed. If its opponents have their way, it will be proscribed again. It may make sense in terms of our system of government that abortion was "illegal" in 1972 and "legal" in 1973, but it's nonsense to say that the same action done by the same people in the same way for the same reasons is "morally right" one year and "morally wrong" the next.

The coercive power of the law or of majority opinion may be able to tell us what we can or can't do with impunity. But it cannot serve as a reliable guide to morality.

Ethics and Religion

As long as we're talking about authority and personal feelings, there's one other issue I want to bring up, and that's religion.

Most people in this country probably associate ideas of right and wrong with religions more than anything else. This is understandable since one of the main functions of religion is to advise people how to live.

Having been religious in a conventional way earlier in my life and now being religious in an unconventional way, I can appreciate how important religions are to people who believe in them. They comfort and protect us in a way that no government, school, business, or other institution can. In the face of human hatred, the threat of nuclear destruction, a universe exploding headlong into infinity, and our own storm-tossed days, religions give us a sense that life isn't quite as bleak as it seems. The world becomes ordered and purposeful, and we have our own special, protected niche. The winds aren't quite so biting, the bumps less jarring.

However, for the sake of learning the skills associated with a philosophical analysis of ethical problems, I'm going to exclude considering a religious approach to ethics for three reasons. First, religious ethics and philosophical ethics are two different enterprises. One is spiritual, the other intellectual. Second, when religions make moral pronouncements, they often speak the language of authority or feeling, which puts it outside the realm of public discussion and philosophical ethics. And third, some people in this country believe that you can't be ethical unless you're religious. I hope to show that this isn't true. Using a philosophical approach to ethics gives you insight into the moral character of actions, reasons for being ethical, and the ability to find some common ground on which to argue intelligently with anyone about controversial issues in morality. After all, while an atheist won't be convinced by the teachings of a spiritual leader or the Bible, he or she will generally listen to secular points and intellectual arguments.

The main problem, however, is that the contributions of particular religions to discussions of right and wrong remain within the flock. Religions are built on faith, and if you don't accept certain fundamental teachings, you won't get much out of the ethical judgments offered by religious figures. Roman Catholic tradition gives considerable moral authority to the Pope, but if you're Lutheran, Jewish, or Buddhist, the Pope's teaching probably doesn't mean very much to you.

Most religious pronouncements about right and wrong, then, are founded on some idea other than that "What counts most is what you think." And for that reason, they're outside the province of philosophical ethics. Philosophical ethics is a decidedly secular enterprise.

This is not to say that religious teachings have nothing to offer to a philosophical discussion. Examining a religion's teachings about sexual morality, for example, may reveal some points that are actually rational and secular. And these are certainly relevant to a philosophical discussion of an ethical dilemma. After all, every reason a spiritual leader gives isn't necessarily strictly religious or spiritual. In fact Chapter 5 (which focuses on why we should worry about the morality of what we do) includes something from one of the great teachers of the Christian church, Saint Augustine. But as a rule, religion and philosophical ethics don't have a lot in common.

CONCLUSION

At this point you may think you know more about what ethics *isn't* than what it *is*. So far I've tried to dispense with some erroneous ideas about ethics. To review quickly, we've seen that:

> Ethics is a branch of philosophy concerned with evaluating how right or wrong human actions are;

Ethics works through making intellectual judgments on the basis of rational explanation and public discussion;

The aim of an ethical argument is to get someone else to freely agree with you for good reasons;

Neither your own emotions nor the authority of individual opinion, the laws, religious teachings, or another person count as much in philosophical ethics as what you think.

DISCUSSION QUESTIONS

1. Describe the similarities and differences among the following statements:
    a. "You can't just punch someone who insults you. It's against the law."
    b. "Honor thy father and thy mother."
    c. "We can't price that product at six dollars. It'll put us in the red."
    d. "I can't go to bed with you. I'll feel too guilty tomorrow."
    e. "You shouldn't take money from your roommate's wallet without asking first. That's wrong."
2. Think of something you believe is a clear case of something *wrong*. Come up with a completely rational and secular argument to explain why.
3. Consider how effectively you could argue with the following people. What would you say to get them to change their minds? Would they change yours? What would your conversations be like? How would you feel in these situations?
    a. A friend who says, "I know I said I'd help you with your paper Saturday, but I've got a really hot date. Look, you'd do the same if you were in my shoes."
    b. A fellow student who says, "Sure I stole that textbook from the bookstore. But tuition's so high at this school, I figured they owed it to me."
    c. Someone who is passionately committed to a particular cause who says, "The only way my people are going to be free is if the world knows we're serious. And they'll know that when we kill some innocent people to make our point. This is war. And some innocent people always die in a war."
    d. A devoutly religious person who believes in the Bible who claims, "God's law is explicit. 'Thou shalt not commit

adultery.' It's clearly wrong. I think that we should make adultery illegal and punish any offenders severely. If we clamp down on adultery we'll be saving the souls of some people who would otherwise commit this terrible sin."

4. Are any of the following people doing anything *morally wrong?*

    a. Luis is sitting at the red traffic light at 2 A.M. There's no traffic around and he can see that no cars are coming from any direction. Luis drives through the red light.

    b. Ann's parents say that she may not date a particular boy. She disobeys them and sees him anyway.

    c. Bill's religion teaches that killing is wrong. He comes upon someone trying to rape his girlfriend. In a furious rage, he kills the attacker.

chapter 2

An "Ethical Yardstick"

I explained in Chapter 1 that ethics' main task is evaluating actions. But what are the terms of the evaluation? What is characteristic of an ethical evaluation? How do we know we have an ethical problem on our hands? How do we separate right from wrong? What makes one action better, or at least less bad, than another?

WHAT MAKES SOMETHING WRONG?

People actually have a much easier time talking about *wrong* than *right*, so let's look at how most people define *wrong*.

If you ask a group of individuals to explain what they believe makes an action *morally wrong*, you may get the following answers: "Something is wrong if it

1. goes against my deepest personal beliefs."
2. hurts somebody."
3. makes me feel guilty."
4. interferes with other people's lives."
5. breaks the laws or traditions of my society."
6. causes physical or emotional harm to someone."
7. violates someone's rights."

Most of us would agree with this commonsense list. It gives us a good place to start, because these different definitions can be divided into three groups. One of the most common ways that people define *wrong* is in terms of the **consequences** or **results** of actions. Definitions 2 (hurting somebody) and 6 (causing physical or emotional harm) explicitly mention hurting or harming other people. Most ordinary, decent people think that there's something not quite right with an action that produces pain, distress, or anguish in someone else. We may believe that in some circumstances it's O.K. to hurt people (as in war or in protecting ourselves against attack). But most of us see that as the exception rather than the rule. We mainly disapprove of actions that make others feel pain.

Other common explanations of *wrong* are in definitions 4 (interfering with other people's lives) and 7 (violating someone's rights). Sometimes you'll hear this put in terms of "forcing people to live under certain restrictions against their will," "controlling" or "manipulating" them, or treating others with "disrespect." But it all amounts to the same thing. What these definitions have in common is that they say that wrong actions don't treat people the way human beings should be treated. These definitions assume that people have "rights" or deserve to be in control of their own lives, and that there's something amiss about actions that don't recognize that. What people are objecting to here, then, aren't the *consequences* of an action as much as something about the action itself. They're saying, "This isn't the kind of action that should take place among fellow humans, no matter what comes from it."

That leaves us with definitions 1 (conflicting with personal beliefs), 3 (feeling guilty), and 5 (violating a society's laws or norms). In Chapter 1, I explained how feelings and laws aren't really within the province of philosophical ethics. But people frequently refer to both of these things in explaining why something is wrong—and with good reason. For in these three definitions we find wrong being defined as anything that violates an ultimate **standard.** The first two definitions refer to an internal, personal guideline—what people sometimes refer to as "conscience" or "personal values." Definition 1 identifies the beliefs themselves; 3 refers to the disappointment most of us feel with ourselves when we go against our own deeply held convictions. The other definition appeals to external norms. But what they share is direct reference to a standard.

An average person, then, would probably present any or all of these three ideas to explain what makes something morally wrong: harmful *consequences,* inappropriate *actions* and behavior that falls short of some important *standard.*

These three ideas present the basic concepts that we're going to explore. When we do philosophical ethics, we apply a special standard to actions and/or the consequences that result from the actions.

The idea of a standard, however, is the most important of the three because that's how we measure the actions and consequences. This standard lets us decide which consequences are *harmful,* and which actions are inappropriate. So if we want to get anywhere in understanding ethics, we have to develop a clear idea of such a basic standard.

THE BASIS OF A STANDARD—HUMAN GOOD

Although the third group of definitions from above implicitly relies on the idea of a standard, they don't really give us much help in discovering a useful "moral yardstick." "Personal beliefs" are as variable as individuals themselves. "Guilt" plagues some people about virtually everything they do; others seem immune to anything remotely resembling remorse. And "laws" and "norms" vary enormously between societies, and they even change within societies.

If we turn to the first two sets of definitions, however, we find quite a bit to work with. After all, people who define *wrong* in terms of harm or pain are referring to something tangible, and the actions that the second group of people rule out are relatively specific—violating someone's rights, manipulating them, and so on. And if we generalize what both groups think, we can say that they defined something *morally wrong* when it produced *human unhappiness.* There are basically two ways that people's lives can be made worse—subjecting them to certain physical conditions (pain) and treating them in certain ways (denying them their rights). The other side of the coin, then, is that if something is *morally right,* it must make people happy, or make their lives better.

This commonsense attitude connecting right and wrong with happiness and unhappiness is virtually identical with the conclusions of the great philosophers on ethics. For despite the heated debate and controversy that accompany ethical dilemmas, the ultimate aim of philosophical ethics is quite simple: to evaluate how much actions will increase or decrease **human happiness, human good** or **human well-being.** To the extent that an action retards, prevents, or minimizes **human good,** we say that it's *morally unjustifiable* or *morally wrong* (or at least morally *worse* than another action). On the other hand, if an action advances, is conducive to, or maximizes *human good,* it's *morally right,* or *morally justifiable* (or at least morally *better* than something else).

The most basic standard used in a philosophical approach to ethics, then, is nothing more sophisticated, mysterious, or complicated than *human good.* Philosophical ethics doesn't judge right and wrong in terms of sacred texts, divine will, subjective beliefs, personal feelings, the word of some authority, laws, or the traditions in a particular culture. Instead it uses a standard that aims to be objective, neutral, rational, public, and secular—whether good or harm is experienced by the people involved, and whether individuals are being treated the way they're entitled to.

There's much to be said for using this kind of a standard for trying to resolve disagreements about ethical issues. It is free of the problems that plague totally personal, emotional standards that can be neither explained nor defended. If we disagree about whether homosexuality is right or wrong, it's pointless for us to trade statements about how we each *feel.* But it would certainly be productive for us to discuss whether homosexuality produces more human good or harm. In the same way, we can use this standard in discussions with people with completely opposite religious beliefs or with no religious beliefs at all. If a Fundamentalist and an atheist disagree about the morality of divorce, they'll obviously get nowhere talking about "God's law." But they can engage in productive dialogue if they focus on whether or not divorce produces more happiness than unhappiness in the lives of the people involved, and whether or not it's ever right for spouses to break their marriage vows.

Appraising in a rational and secular manner whether or not actions or policies foster human happiness has been the goal of ethics since its beginning 2,000 years ago in the dusty streets of Athens. There's been no debate about the aim of ethics. If *human happiness* or *human well-being* is at stake, we've got a moral or ethical issue. It's that simple.

The hard part is to define human happiness or human well-being, and getting people to agree on it. In this chapter we're going to try to develop a commonsense idea of human happiness with which most people will agree. On the basis of that we can fashion a kind of rough "ethical yardstick"—a standard we can use to see how actions measure up.

So What's "Happiness"?

Happiness is one of my least favorite terms in ethics because it is misleading to the modern ear. When you talk about *happiness,* people seem to think you mean something emotional. As when I say, "I'm so happy to see you!" or "I'm so happy I got that job!" In these cases we're talking about gladness or joy—two reputable emotions, but not what we have in mind in ethics.

I prefer terms like *human good, human well-being, human satisfaction* or *human fulfillment.* Even though it's so much longer, *a state of full human development* seems better to me than *happiness.* Any of these terms conveys better what we're talking about because *fulfillment, satisfaction* and *well-being* at least suggest quieter and richer states than *happiness.* They also bring to mind more things that can go into making us feel that way. So what we're talking about isn't some passing emotional state when you feel really "up" or "high." It's a more general sense of completeness or contentment with life. Our basic needs are met; we feel relatively safe and secure; our life is free of serious turmoil and anguish. We may not be experiencing any great emotional highs and our life may not be filled with great pleasure, but we have a general sense that life is fundamentally O.K. and free of pain.

The key to this notion is the word *human*. When philosphers refer to "human happiness or well-being" we mean a general state of satisfaction or fulfillment with life that is uniquely human. We assume that human beings are special creatures, different from any other on earth, and that they can enjoy in a unique way the pleasures of being human.

Take freedom, for example. If I turned my friend's golden retriever loose saying, "I hereby release you from bondage! Be free! Enjoy your liberty!" I wouldn't make her life any better. In fact, I might make it worse because now she'd have a harder time finding food and protection. If I liberated a human being, however, I'd improve his life by quantum leaps. People need and enjoy the ability to run their own lives in a way that dogs, cats, squirrels, or gerbils don't. We enjoy it in a way denied to any other species. We may be able to domesticate cats, but the instinct for liberty is so strong in humans that we'll never successfully domesticate one another. So human happiness, human well-being, or human good refers to a state of affairs brought about by our distinctly human needs being met.

HUMAN NEEDS

This approach to ethics believes that there are basics that we all need in order to be satisfied in life just because we're human. Happiness, satisfaction, well-being or fulfillment is the state of general contentment we'd be in if we had all of the basic things that we really need.

So what is it that we all need in order to have that sense of contentment? The most obvious needs are things like food, shelter, protection, and physical heath. But there are many more. One of the best descriptions of all of them, however, is a document adopted by the United Nations called the *"Universal Declaration of Human Rights."* (For the complete document see Figure 1.)

Figure 1   Universal Declaration of Human Rights

Preamble

Whereas recognition of the inherent dignity and of the equal and inalienable rights of all members of the human family is the foundation of freedom, justice and peace in the world,

Whereas disregard and contempt for human rights have resulted in barbarous acts which have outraged the conscience of mankind, and the advent of a world in which human beings shall enjoy freedom of speech and belief and freedom from fear and want has been proclaimed as the highest aspiration of the common people,

Whereas it is essential, if man is not to be compelled to have recourse, as a last resort, to rebellion against tyranny and oppression, that human rights should be protected by the rule of law,

Whereas it is essential to promote the development of friendly relations between nations,

Whereas the peoples of the United Nations have in the Charter reaffirmed their faith in fundamental human rights, in the dignity and worth of the human person and in the equal rights of men and women and have determined to promote social progress and better standards of life in larger freedom,

Whereas Member States have pledged themselves to achieve, in cooperation with the United Nations, the promotion of universal respect for and observance of human rights and fundamental freedoms,

Whereas a common understanding of these rights and freedoms is of the greatest importance for the full realization of this pledge,

Now, Therefore,
The General Assembly

proclaims
This Universal Declaration of Human Rights

as a common standard of achievement for all peoples and nations, to the end that every individual and every organ of society, keeping this Declaration constantly in mind, shall strive by teaching and education to promote respect for these rights and freedoms and by progressive measures, national and international, to secure their universal and effective recognition and observance, both among the peoples of Member States themselves and among the peoples of territories under their jurisdiction.

Article 1

All human beings are born free and equal in dignity and rights. They are endowed with reason and conscience and should act towards one another in a spirit of brotherhood.

Article 2

Everyone is entitled to all the rights and freedoms set forth in this Declaration, without distinction of any kind, such as race, colour, sex, language, religion, political or other opinion, national or social origin, property, birth or other status.

Furthermore, no distinction shall be made on the basis of the political, jurisdictional or international status of the country or territory to which a person belongs, whether it be independent, trust, non-selfgoverning or under any other limitation of sovereignty.

Article 3

Everyone has the right to life, liberty and security of person.

Article 4

No one shall be held in slavery or servitude; slavery and the slave trade shall be prohibited in all their forms.

Article 5

No one shall be subjected to torture or to cruel, inhuman or degrading treatment or punishment.

Article 6

Everyone has the right to recognition everywhere as a person before the law.

Article 7

All are equal before the law and are entitled without any discrimination to equal protection of the law. All are entitled to equal protection against any discrimination in violation of this Declaration and against any incitement to such discrimination.

Article 8

Everyone has the right to an effective remedy by the competent national tribunals for acts violating the fundamental rights granted him by the constitution or by law.

Article 9

No one shall be subjected to arbitrary arrest, detention or exile.

Article 10

Everyone is entitled in full equality to a fair and public hearing by an independent and impartial tribunal, in the determination of his rights and obligations and of any criminal charge against him.

Article 11

(1) Everyone charged with a penal offence has the right to be presumed innocent until proved guilty according to law in a public trial at which he has had all the guarantees necessary for his defence.

(2) No one shall be held guilty of any penal offence on account of any act or omission which did not constitute a penal offence, under national or international law, at the time when it was committed. Nor shall a heavier penalty be imposed than the one that was applicable at the time the penal offence was committed.

Article 12

No one shall be subjected to arbitrary interference with his privacy, family, home or correspondence, nor to attacks upon his honour and reputation. Everyone has the right to the protection of the law against such interference or attacks.

Article 13

(1) Everyone has the right to freedom of movement and residence within the borders of each State.

(2) Everyone has the right to leave any country, including his own, and to return to his country.

Article 14

(1) Everyone has the right to seek and to enjoy in other countries asylum from persecution.

(2) This right may not be invoked in the case of prosecutions genuinely arising from non-political crimes or from acts contrary to the purposes and principles of the United Nations.

Article 15

(1) Everyone has the right to a nationality.

(2) No one shall be arbitrarily deprived of his nationality nor denied the right to change his nationality.

Article 16

(1) Men and women of full age, without any limitation due to race, nationality or religion, have the right to marry and to found a family. They are entitled to equal rights as to marriage, during marriage and at its dissolution.

(2) Marriage shall be entered into only with the free and full consent of the intending spouses.

(3) The family is the natural and fundamental group unit of society and is entitled to protection by society and the State.

Article 17

(1) Everyone has the right to own property alone as well as in association with others.

(2) No one shall be arbitrarily deprived of his property.

Article 18

Everyone has the right to freedom of thought, conscience and religion; this right includes freedom to change his religion or belief, and freedom, either alone or in community with others and in public or private, to manifest his religion or belief in teaching, practice, worship and observance.

Article 19

Everyone has the right to freedom of opinion and expression; this right includes freedom to hold opinions without interference and to seek, receive and impart information and ideas through any media and regardless of frontiers.

Article 20

(1) Everyone has the right to freedom of peaceful assembly and association.

(2) No one may be compelled to belong to an association.

Article 21

(1) Everyone has the right to take part in the government of his country, directly or through freely chosen representatives.

(2) Everyone has the right of equal access to public service in his country.

(3) The will of the people shall be the basis of the authority of government; this will shall be expressed in periodic and genuine elections which shall be by universal and equal suffrage and shall be held by secret vote or by equivalent free voting procedures.

Article 22

Everyone, as a member of society, has the right to social security and is entitled to realization, through national effort and international co-operation and in accordance with the organization and resources of each State, of the economic, social and cultural rights indispensable for his dignity and the free development of his personality.

Article 23

(1) Everyone has the right to work, to free choice of employment, to just and favourable conditions of work and to protection against unemployment.

(2) Everyone, without any discrimination, has the right to equal pay for equal work.

(3) Everyone who works has the right to just and favourable remuneration ensuring for himself and his family an existence worthy of human dignity, and supplemented, if necessary, by other means of social protection.

Article 24

Everyone has the right to rest and leisure, including reasonable limitation of working hours and periodic holidays with pay.

Article 25

(1) Everyone has the right to a standard of living adequate for the health and well-being of himself and of his family, including food, clothing, housing and medical care and necessary social services, and the right to security in the event of unemployment, sickness, disability, widowhood, old age or other lack of livelihood in circumstances beyond his control.

(2) Motherhood and childhood are entitled to special care and assistance. All children, whether born in or out of wedlock, shall enjoy the same social protection.

Article 26

(1) Everyone has the right to education. Education shall be free, at least in the elementary and fundamental stages. Elementary education shall be compulsory. Technical and professional education shall be made generally available and higher education shall be equally accessible to all on the basis of merit.

(2) Education shall be directed to the full development of the human personality and to the strengthening of respect for human rights and fundamental freedoms. It shall promote understanding, tolerance and friendship among all nations, racial or religious groups, and shall further the activities of the United Nations for the maintenance of peace.

(3) Parents have a prior right to choose the kind of education that shall be given to their children.

Article 27

(1) Everyone has the right freely to participate in the cultural life of the community, to enjoy the arts and to share in scientific advancement and its benefits.

(2) Everyone has the right to the protection of the moral and material interests resulting from any scientific, literary or artistic production of which he is the author.

Article 28

Everyone is entitled to a social and international order in which the rights and freedoms set forth in this Declaration can be fully realized.

Article 29

(1) Everyone has duties to the community in which alone the free and full development of his personality is possible.

(2) In the exercise of his rights and freedoms, everyone shall be subject only to such limitations as are determined by law solely for the purpose of securing due recognition and respect for the rights and freedoms of others and of meeting the just requirements of morality, public order and the general welfare in a democratic society.

(3) These rights and freedoms may in no case be exercised contrary to the purposes and principles of the United Nations.

Article 30

Nothing in this Declaration may be interpreted as implying for any State, group or person any right to engage in any activity or to perform any act aimed at the destruction of any of the rights and freedoms set forth herein.

(Reprinted with permission of the United Nations. The Universal Declaration of Human Rights of the United Nations, *General Assembly resolution 217 A(III) of 10 December 1948.)*

This document refers to "rights" but it may as well say "needs." The theory it's based on maintains that we have a "right" to something if we "need" it in a special, fundamental way. The document's thirty articles list basic and important things that all of us as humans need to experience a satisfying, contented life. Or, to put it another way, the more of these things we're deprived of, the less our chances of being fully satisfied with our lives.

There's nothing especially novel or fancy about this list of "rights" or "needs." The document is very detailed and broken down into a preamble and thirty articles, but in essence it lists only very basic things: life itself, freedom, equality, personal security, protection by a just legal system, political rights, a private life, the ability to choose marriage and family, freedom of thought and action, access to the benefits of a society (government, culture, education, protection against illness), work, and rest.

The most basic point to understand about this document is that it describes the needs of "all peoples and all nations." It assumes that the conditions it describes are as objectively necessary for human happiness as the conditions needed for human health.

For example, let's look at Article 3, "Everyone has the right to life, liberty, and security of person." Imagine what it would be like if your "life, liberty, and security of person" were constantly at risk. You'd always fear being killed, enslaved, or attacked. You couldn't trust anyone because you wouldn't know who was a friend and who a foe. Your life would be filled with worry and dread, and you'd probably be plotting against the people you thought were most dangerous to you. Such a way of life is hardly appealing.

Now because humans are so adaptable, in one way or another most of us could adjust to such a way of life. But could you imagine any normal person actually feeling good about life under these conditions? Could you imagine any normal individual even feeling calm and untroubled—never mind feeling good? Human beings—no matter what the traditions or norms of their culture—don't experience deep fear about losing their lives or liberty as satisfying. If you injected such fear into the average day of an ordinary person, in one stroke you'd dramatically diminish how much he or she enjoyed life.

Or consider the first part of Article 26, "Everyone has the right to education. Education shall be free, at least in the elementary and fundamental stages. Elementary education shall be compulsory. Technical and professional education shall be made generally available and higher education shall be equally accessible to all on the basis of merit." This provision asserts that everyone has a right to education because human beings need education in order to live a decent life. How satisfying do you think you or anyone else would find life if you were barred from learning how to read and write or prohibited from developing any but the simplest skills? You would feel unfulfilled, frustrated, and bored. Your life would be devastatingly empty, void of any significant challenges. Or it would be a torment in which your lack of knowledge and skills would condemn you to fail at virtually anything you tried to do.

And again, no matter what part of the world people live in, no matter what the traditions of their culture, no ordinary human being is going to experience anything but frustration and dissatisfaction at being deprived of the opportunity to develop his or her abilities.

It's also important to notice that despite how many specific conditions are listed throughout the thirty articles, we can lump them into two categories. First, many of the articles refer to specific *material* or *physical* conditions. The Declaration says humans need things like: life, liberty, security of person, freedom of movement, freedom of assembly, a certain standard of living, work, education, and rest. It also identifies material conditions that men and women need protection against: slavery, torture, interference with their private lives, and the like. Obviously, the first set makes our lives more pleasant, the second more painful.

But the articles also talk about acceptable and unacceptable procedures or ways of treating people. We're told we have rights to: equality before the law, fairness, a presumption of innocence, impartial tribunals, marriages based only on consent, and equal pay for equal work. And we're entitled to be protected against: discrimination, arbitrary arrest, being accused of an offense that wasn't a crime when we did it, arbitrarily being deprived of our property, and so on. These articles don't care about the consequences of such actions; it wouldn't make any difference that good results could come from some of these things. (After all, some people believe you end up with less crime in a society if you presume that someone charged with a crime is guilty and put the burden on him to establish his innocence.) What's at stake here are principles—equality, justice, fairness, respect for individual liberty—which are supposed to guide our actions independent of the likely outcome. The Declaration assumes that no amount of good could offset the harm produced by breaking these principles because some actions are just intrinsically wrong. That is, this way of thinking sees actions that are unfair, arbitrary, discriminatory, biased, or unjust as simply in and of themselves unacceptable and inconsistent tent with human happiness or well-being.

When you look over this document you may find that you don't totally agree with it. Perhaps you think people could be perfectly happy without some of these things. Or maybe there are some needs you'd like added. But the idea to focus on isn't so much the Declaration's details as the assumption it's built on—that we can describe both the material conditions and rules or principles of human behavior that would have to be met in order for any normal man or woman to live a satisfying life.

Needs and Morality

You'll remember, however, that the point of this discussion about human needs or rights is to try to develop and illustrate a basic standard of morality. So when we say in philosophical ethics that the things that encourage human good are morally better than the things that retard it, we can think of something like the "Universal Declaration of Human Rights" (or any statement of the necessary conditions for human happiness) as an ethical yardstick. Actions or policies that measure up, that is, that let people enjoy the conditions listed or treat them with appropriate respect, are "right" or "morally superior" because they increase human happiness or are consistent with human well-being. Actions that fall short, that is, that keep people from having these basic needs met or simply treat them inappropriately, are "wrong" or "morally inferior" because they make people's lives less satisfying.

Starting in the next chapter, we'll see that philosophers debate about just how you measure human happiness, and we'll look at a couple of variations on the ethical yardstick. But even in the midst of serious disagreement, nobody abandons either the basic idea that you can specify the conditions that people need in order to be satisfied, or the fundamental notion that these are the things you look at in determining the moral character of actions.

SOMETHING FOR THE SKEPTICS

I know from experience that some of you aren't buying this. You may think, "Different people need different things to be happy. Individuals go after what they decide will make them happy or they just follow the dictates of their culture. Just look around. People and cultures are different. You can't say everybody needs the same things to be happy."

There's an element of truth here, but not enough to overthrow this whole theory. Obviously, different men and women value different things. Some seek money, success, or power; others prefer fame to wealth. Some dedicate themselves to a cause; others place their families at the center of their lives. Similarly, western Europe and the United States enjoy fairly open attitudes toward sex, while kissing in public is scandalous in China. Some societies recognize the equality between the sexes, while others are rigidly chauvinistic. But all this shows is that different individuals and cultures are trying different ways to reach the same end—a sense of satisfaction with life.

Some variety in what people seek is to be expected. After all, one of the most basic things that humans need is freedom—the ability to choose how we're going to live as individuals. However, variety alone doesn't prove that every option is as good as the other. The diversity may mean that lots of people are really off track. In other words, just because people *want* something and *believe* it will make them happy doesn't mean that it will.

Let's approach this matter another way. Think of your body and then the bodies of people around you. Despite the individual differences, all human bodies are similar. They're biological engines. In order to run, they need to take in various substances: protein, carbohydrates, vitamins, minerals. Everybody should also get exercise. When everything is working right, your body is operating the way it's supposed to—a condition we call *health*. Health is the proper condition of a human body. Bodies that fall short of this standard are at best "out of shape" or "weak," at worst they're diseased or ill.

Medical science can describe health and disease in remarkable detail independently of our opinion on the matter. To take a simple example, we know the range of a normal heartbeat (60 to 100 beats per minute) and that a blood pressure reading of 120 over 70 is optimum. If I consistently run a reading of 180 over 110, however, I'll be diagnosed as hypertensive and treated for the disease. I may feel fine and think I'm healthy, but I'd be mistaken. My body has the final word on the matter. No matter what I believe or want to tell myself, a sedentary life and high cholesterol intake will gradually produce obstructions in my circulatory system. My body is diseased and I'm on my way to a heart attack unless I mend my ways. Still, the choice is mine.

The same thing applies to smoking. No matter what any individual smoker believes, smoking cigarettes does not help the body's health. Even if years of smoking don't bring on lung cancer, there's a good chance they'll lead to respiratory or circulatory ailments. This is simply the result of the interaction between human tissue and cigarette smoke. The opinion of the smoker is totally irrelevant to the outcome.

However, if you're a smoker, you probably feel that the short-term pleasures of smoking outweigh the long-term risks. And that's why you choose to continue smoking. We all have the power to act against our own long-term interests. And most of us do so about one thing or another (whether it be alcohol, drugs, or just a really poor diet), believing we have good reason to act as we do. Nonetheless, whatever we believe isn't going to change the fact that what we're doing—in a clear cut and objective way— is ultimately not going to help our bodies. We may *feel* better for now, but we won't *be* better in the end.

Or take this example.* Imagine that a hitherto unknown village is discovered high in the Andes, that the people agree to be examined by physicians from the United Nations, and that we're all part of the group. We stay with these people for a month observing their way of life and doing scores of sophisticated medical tests on them. Let's say we discover that these people are living under the worst possible conditions. Their

*I owe this example to Professor Robert Paul Wolff.

land produces very poor crops; their water supply is filled with disease-producing micro-organisms; they have a terrible diet; they suffer from chronic malnutrition and anemia; their condition has weakened their bones and muscles; their brains may also be affected; and most of them die by age fifty. In short, they are all unhealthy.

Imagine that we then report our findings to their council of elders hoping to encourage them to move to a better location. How do you think they'd react to the news that they're all sick? At first they probably won't believe us. They may accept that *some* of their people are sick or weak, but not *all* of them. Also, they're the council of *elders*. By definition they've lived long lives (although by our count not a one is over forty-five). Furthermore and most importantly, they tell us about a village that's higher in the mountains and faced with even worse conditions. In relation to the people of this other village, they consider themselves strong, robust, and long-lived.

Now it's possible that we might ultimately be able to convince them of our findings, but that really doesn't matter for our discussion. What's important is that these people have developed a conception of health from their own experiences and most likely will strongly resist the idea that their entire society is ill. Nonetheless, despite what they believe, in fact they are unhealthy in terms of what we know is a standard definition of human health in the late twentieth century.

Although we can't draw a precise parallel between physical health and human happiness, the parallel is close enough to entertain seriously. That is, in the same way that everybody needs pretty much the same things to be healthy, every human being seems to need roughly the same things in order to have a basic sense of contentment or satisfaction with life. That's just the way the human being in general is designed. It enjoys certain things; it's pained by other conditions. Whether or not someone believes that people need freedom of opinion is as immaterial as whether or not she believes that her diet is far too rich in salt. Too much salt will eventually make her less healthy. Anyone being denied freedom of opinion is being deprived of something that would make their lives more satisfying. What we need to be happy is determined by the fabric out of which we're all made.

On Human Adaptability

The real skeptics among you may be thinking, "What about the fact that cultures differ so much and that humans can adapt so readily to different conditions? What about slavery? Lots of slave owners treated their slaves well. Surely many of them must have been happy. Or look at the people today who can't make a decision and are happiest when someone else tells them what to do. Liberty or being in control of their own lives only makes them *un*happy."

Well, it's true that humans are marvelously adaptable and that some slave owners were decent to their slaves. But even though people can get used to servitude, their lives would be even more satisfying if they were free. There may be benefits which partially compensate for the loss of freedom—not having to worry about providing for yourself, having a kind of guaranteed employment—but they can never balance out the loss of liberty. And, though people can adapt to all sorts of circumstances, some conditions are simply not consistent with the idea of full human development.

A variation on this argument involves people who seem happiest when someone else is making decisions for them. They may feel content inside, but they're not experiencing the deeper satisfactions that come from running their own lives. Dependent people live like children; some part of them is immature, undeveloped. Their satisfaction is characteristic of a less developed human being. Given your choice, would you rather be a happy, but dependent child or a slightly disgruntled, but competent adult?

Some of you may still believe that we can't make any kind of general statement about what all people need to be happy. But hardly anyone really believes this, and I'll show you why.

Let's go back to the example of the village in the Andes. Let's say that the villagers refuse to move. What would you think about forcing them to—picking them up bodily and transporting them against their willl to another location?

There's hardly anyone who would approve of this. As long as the villagers are aware of the situation, most of us would think it would be wrong to force our will on them. Why? Because most people, especially skeptics, believe that we should respect their right to decide how they want to live their lives. That is, most people believe that—if nothing else—all human beings need the freedom to decide their own fates in order to be satisfied with their lives. Almost everyone who says you can't generalize about this matter ultimately believes that a person's individuality has to be protected.

WHAT MAKES SOMETHING AN "ETHICAL" ISSUE?

In the course of talking about how human good is a standard of right and wrong, we've also given ourselves a way of knowing when an issue is ethical. Whenever human good is on the line, we've got an ethical issue.

Whenever a situation involves any of the conditions for human happiness or well-being, it has an ethical dimension. And human good is involved whenever it touches on basic human needs.

This means, then, that there are roughly two ways we can find ourselves with an ethical issue. Either it involves fulfilling our material needs (some actual good or harm) or it relates to how we're being treated. Stealing the rent money from a senior citizen has more than just a legal dimension. The fact that this money's needed to provide this individual with shelter makes it an ethical issue. Tricking a friend into doing something he or she doesn't want to do is an ethical issue because we generally take personal freedom and control over our actions to be a basic need. If a case involves actual material good or harm, or a question of the appropriateness of how people are being treated, it has an ethical dimension. Understanding an ethical yardstick, then, gives us a way of recognizing ethical problems and evaluating how ethically appropriate particular actions or policies are.

CONCLUSION

In this chapter, we've looked at some of the basic ideas that support a philosophical approach to ethics:

One of the most basic concepts involved in distinguishing right from wrong is a standard used to evaluate the *consequences* of actions or the *actions themselves;*

This basic standard is usually taken to be human happiness, satisfaction or well-being;

Thus, the most fundamental understanding of *morally wrong* is preventing or restricting human happiness, while *morally right* is advancing or maximizing human happiness;

This approach assumes that we can specify the conditions needed for "a generally satisfying human life" in the same way we can detail the criteria for "physical health"; that is, that the ultimate criteria for human happiness are objective and universal;

In identifying the criteria for human happiness we arrive at a list of the most basic human needs and rights (we have a right to something because we need it to live a basically satisfying human life); such a list is a basic ethical standard;

We have an ethical issue, then, when any of these needs (material conditions for human happiness or the need to be treated in a certain way) is on the line.

DISCUSSION QUESTIONS

1. What's your reaction to the idea that right and wrong can be defined entirely in terms of human good and human needs—without any reference to laws, emotions, or religion?

2. What do you think of the general idea that all humans need roughly the same things to live happily?

3. What's your reaction to the United Nations' "Universal Declaration of Human Rights"? Do you think it's an accurate description of the needs of "all members of the human family"? Does it contain anything that you think humans can easily live without? Does it miss anything?

4. Article 23 (2) says, "Everyone, without any discrimination, has the right to equal pay for equal work." Does that mean that before the Equal Pay Act of 1963, which put the notion of "equal pay for equal work" into U.S. law, American companies who paid men and women different salaries for the same job were doing something unethical, although it was legal?

5. Explain why each of the following is an ethical issue. In precisely what way does each involve human good?

    a. You find a wallet on the street. It contains $1,000 in cash and you can tell that this is the wallet of a wealthy man. You return the wallet, but keep the cash thinking that losing the money won't hurt this man a bit (and you're probably right).

    b. You agree to buy alcohol for a fellow student who's underage in your state. You know that this person will get drunk and may then drive.

    c. You're living away at college, but you have a boyfriend/girlfriend back home. You've agreed not to date other people, but you start seeing someone on campus. You don't say anything about breaking your word because you figure that what your sweetheart at home doesn't know won't hurt him/her.

chapter **3**

Measuring Consequences

In the last chapter I tried to develop an ethical yardstick—a standard we can use to gauge the moral worth of actions. Building on the concept of human good or human happiness, Chapter 2's main idea is that the more something meets people's fundamental needs, treats people the way they're entitled to be treated, improves their lives, and increases their sense of basic contentment and satisfaction in life, the better it is from an ethical standpoint. Conversely, to the extent that an action or policy decreases or makes such satisfaction more difficult, it is morally worse.

We also saw that the United Nations' "Universal Declaration of Human Rights" is a convenient description of the fundamental needs of everyone in the human family. The Declaration essentially says that in order to be fully content with life as human beings we need two things— to experience certain material conditions or actual states of affairs (food, shelter, education, the absence of fear) and to be treated in a certain way (equal to others and with fairness). And this echoes the two major ways we saw that people describe what they believe makes something wrong— hurting others (actual state of affairs) and violating someone's rights (treatment).

Actually, these two-fold distinctions represent the two basic ways philosophical ethics measures how much an action makes people's lives better or worse. The approach we're going to look at in this chapter says we discover the moral character of an action (just how morally right or wrong it is) by looking at the *results* or *consequences* it produces. The other approach, which we'll see in Chapter 4, says that we should examine instead the action itself.

A TELEOLOGICAL (RESULTS-ORIENTED) APPROACH TO ETHICS

This handbook will avoid philosophical jargon as much as possible and present ideas in a straightforward, commonsense way. But there will be times when a technical term will help clarify the issue at hand. This is one of them.

Evaluating the moral status of an action by looking at its consequences is one of the most basic, longstanding approaches in philosophical ethics. It has come to be known as the **teleological** approach. Teleological comes from two ancient Greek words: *telos* and *logos*. The latter crops up in lots of modern words and can be taken to mean something like "the study of." *Biology* means "the study of life"; *psychology*, "the study of the psyche"; *sociology*, "the study of society"; *criminology*, "the study of criminal behavior." *Telos* appears very infrequently in English and in this context means "end." So *teleology* means "the study of ends." (To avoid confusion, remember that "end" here means "the end of an action," its "result" or "outcome.") Any approach that says an action is justified by what it produces—even something as crude as the idea that "the ends justify the means"—is basically teleological.

In one respect, a teleological or *results-oriented* approach is one of the most practical and uncomplicated ways to evaluate actions. In a sense it's also scientific. To determine how morally right or wrong an action is, we simply look at the actual results and see how they measure up against our ethical yardstick. How much actual good or happiness is produced? If there's more good than harm, the action is morally O.K.

On the face of it, such an approach makes a lot of sense. Pleasure makes life better. Pain makes it worse. In developing a standard for evaluating human behavior, it makes more sense that "pleasure" belongs with "right" and "pain" with "wrong" than the other way around. Why would we want an ethical guideline that says people should do things that make them unhappy or hurt one another?

This way of thinking also seems sensible and useful. It gives us a commonsense way to resolve moral dilemmas. Instead of debating whether homosexuality is "natural" or "perverse," a teleological approach says we should observe how much actual good or harm it produces. If it leads to more good than harm, it's morally justifiable; if more harm than good, it's unjustifiable. This is like a philosophical application of that saying in sports—"no harm, no foul." If no harm is done, why should we say something is morally wrong?

But measuring how much human good or harm is produced by actions is not as easy as it seems. If we want to make a decision before we do something (the situation we're usually in when we have an ethical dilemma on our hands), we have no actual results to examine. That means we have to imagine likely outcomes and speculate about the odds attached to different options. If we're going to do a complete and accurate job, we need to know what to look for. The "Universal Declaration of Human Rights" might be a place to start, since it tells us that the more the things on the list are produced, the happier people will be. But the Declaration is a political, not a philosophical document, and it takes us only so far. We need something more rigorous and systematic.

Not surprisingly, some philosophers have developed such systems. In this chapter we're going to look at two of them (those of Jeremy Bentham and John Stuart Mill) and see how well they work.

JEREMY BENTHAM, UTILITARIANISM AND PLEASURE

Given the practical and scientific character of a teleological or results-oriented approach to ethics, it's no surprise that one of its strongest advocates is a very practical, empirically oriented individual. And such was Englishman Jeremy Bentham (1748–1832).

Bentham was a practical soul, more reformer than philosopher. He trained in law, but was more concerned with reforming the laws and penal code than being a barrister. Nonetheless, he was seriously interested in the British philosophers of his time who argued for the value of **empiricism,** the basic approach of modern science. In determining how people should behave and in evaluating laws, policies, and institutions, Bentham thought the best approach was to see what produced the most practical good and improved the lives of the most people. Arguing especially against aristocrats who held fast to the authority of tradition, and prelates who praised self-sacrifice and the denial of pleasure and comfort, Bentham became the chief exponent of a theory called **utilitarianism.**

The word *utilitarianism* is obviously built on *utility* which means "usefulness." Bentham thought we should evaluate things simply on how useful they were in improving life. In fact, living by his ideas, Bentham directed that when he died his body should be dissected for the benefit of science. This was much more useful than simply discarding it. Indeed, because Bentham left all of his estate to the University of London on the condition that his remains be present at its board meetings, Bentham's body was stuffed and is on display in a glass case at University College.

Don't think Bentham would be offended by this. One time while in London I was to meet a scholar from the University for lunch. When I called my colleague to find out where we should meet, she said, "Meet me at twelve in front of Jeremy Bentham." It turns out that Bentham's body is the standard meeting place at the University, a fact that would delight Bentham. A century and a half after his death, his body is still "useful."

Utilitarianism is a moral theory, however, not just a general approach to life. So its idea of utility is quite specific and directly related to human happiness. And for Jeremy Bentham what makes human life happy or satisfying is pleasure.

In his *Introduction to the Principles of Morals and Legislation,* Bentham writes, "Nature has placed mankind under the governance of two sovereign masters, *pain* and *pleasure.* It is for them alone to point out what we ought to do. . . . [T]he standard of right and wrong. . .[is] fastened to their throne. . . . By utility is meant that property in any object whereby it tends to produce benefit, advantage, pleasure, good, or happiness (all this in the present case comes to the same thing) or (what comes again to the same thing) to prevent the happening of mischief, pain, evil, or unhappiness to the party whose interest is considered: if that party be the community in general, then the happiness of the community: if a particular individual, then the happiness of that individual."

As far as utilitarianism is concerned, something is morally good to the extent that it produces a greater balance of pleasure over pain for the largest number of people involved, or, "the greatest good of the greatest number." Bentham thinks it's so obvious that pleasure is the ultimate stuff of human happiness, and thus the ultimate standard of human good, that it's ridiculous even to try to prove this point. In Bentham's eyes this is the ultimate, objective standard of morality—"the greatest happiness of all those whose interest is in question [is] the right and proper, and only right and proper and universally desirable, end of human action." We could thus say that Bentham's ethical yardstick is marked off in units of pleasure and held only against the consequences of actions.

Measuring Pleasure—Bentham's "Hedonistic Calculus"

Bentham tells us that if we want to determine the moral character of an action, we should see how much pleasure it produces. Intuitively, this idea seems to make sense. It involves an open, objective and public process of measuring pleasure. It's very democratic—everybody is equal and the pleasures of the majority prevail. And pleasure is something everybody understands. There's nothing fancy or mysterious about it. So far so good.

But how do you measure pleasure? How do we weigh pleasure against pain? Systematic and practical man that he was, Jeremy Bentham gives us a way—the **hedonistic calculus.**

The *hedonistic calculus* is a system that lets us measure and compare the amounts of pleasure and pain that different actions produce. (*Hedonistic* comes from the Greek word for "pleasure.") Bentham identifies seven elements that we have to take into account: (1) the *intensity* of the feeling; (2) its *duration;* (3) its *certainty* or *uncertainty;* (4) its *propinquity* or *remoteness* (how soon we'll experience it); (5) its *fecundity* (the likelihood that the experience will produce other pleasures in the future); (6) its *purity* (the chance the feeling will produce pain or unhappiness); and (7) its *extent* (the number of people affected by it). The object of the game is to assign a numerical value to each of these categories for each of the actions or options we're measuring, tally them up, and compare the final scores. Whichever has the higher total is morally better.

Let's take three different cases and see how well Bentham's system works.

Example 1: Mugging Grandma

Imagine that your car has just broken down and it's going to take five hundred dollars to repair it—five hundred dollars that you don't have. Since you desperately need your car for work and school, you try to borrow the money from family, friends, and associates, but come up dry. Next you try a bank, but here too you have no luck. You have no credit history and no collateral. As you go to leave the bank, however, you spy this little old lady taking a wad of bills from one of the tellers and stuffing them into her purse. At first you just feel depressed about life's unfairness and your predicament. You're sure your boss is going to fire you and that you'll miss classes to boot. But as you're walking home, you realize that this little old lady is walking along the same *deserted* street that you are. You look around and see no one else around and—a victim of your despair—wonder whether you should steal this woman's purse. There's the dilemma: Do you steal the money or not?

Most people would be hard pressed to say that mugging a little old lady is "morally right," so Bentham's calculus should come to the same conclusion. We have to take each of the seven categories and assign a number that tells how much pleasure or pain is involved, so let's use a scale of -10 to $+10$. Positive numbers will stand for pleasurable feelings, negative numbers unpleasant ones. To see whether mugging Grandma will produce more pleasure than pain, let's compare the theft's effects on the little old lady versus the effects on you.

	Grandma	**You**
1. Intensity	−10	+2

How intense is the experience for each of you? Being mugged is a very intense, totally unpleasant experience. So −10 should describe your victim's feelings. Coming up with a score for you is more complicated because so many more feelings are involved. If you're normal, the experience will probably be pretty intense, but it will involve both good and bad feelings. You're apprehensive about taking the money and getting away without being seen, caught, or hurting the woman. Your heart will be pounding (a sure sign of intensity) and you may feel really guilty about what you've done. So that looks like about a −8 for you. But once you think you've escaped and know that you can get your car fixed, you'll probably be very happy. For the time being, you've saved your job and you can continue in school. For the sake of argument, let's assume that your happiness will be very intense (+10). So, on balance you'll feel more intensely happy than unhappy by +2.

2. Duration	−10	−2

How long will the pleasure or pain last? Again, it's easy to come up with a value for your victim. Being mugged isn't something you easily get over. The intensity will decrease, but the woman will feel unhappy about this for a long time (−10). Your happiness won't last as long—only until you need money again or your car breaks down (let's say +6). But you'll probably also be feeling some guilt, or at least some bad feelings about having been put in a position where stealing was your only way out. And you may also be worrying about whether you'll eventually be caught. Those feelings will probably last longer than the happy ones. Depending on how much of a conscience you have, you might be haunted by the event for the rest of your life. Let's assign a −8 for your negative feelings, which gives you a −2 on balance.

3. Certainty	−10	+7

What's the likelihood that the pleasure or pain we think will result from the event actually will? There's no question that Grandma is going to feel bad about this—whether you get away with the theft or not (−10). What are the odds that you'll feel good? Probably a little less (+7). You've got to get away with the crime first and then you'll likely have mixed feelings.

    4. Propinquity   −10   +8

How soon? Your victim is going to start feeling bad immediately. You're going to have to wait until you know you've escaped unrecognized or maybe even until you get your car fixed.

    5. Fecundity   +1   +10

How likely is it that the theft is going to produce more pleasure in the future? Hardly any chance of that for the little old lady. However, since friends or family would probably give her at least some care and support, we'd probably better say +1. On the other hand, the odds are really good for you. You're getting yourself out of financial trouble. You'll get your car repaired, keep your job, not fall behind in your classes, and so on. That's a fair amount of happiness. Let's say +10. (Scores on fecundity can only be positive since all they measure are future pleasures. Scores for purity, the next category, take care of the other side of the coin and can only be negative.)

    6. Purity   −8   −4

How likely is it that the theft will lead to future unhappiness? Very likely for your victim. The memory will make her upset. She'll worry more often about being mugged. She'll probably go to some trouble to make sure it doesn't happen again. It may not be heart-wrenching, intense unhappiness, but it won't be insignificant. Let's say −8. What about you? Guilt, remorse, future worry about getting caught. Some unhappiness, but probably not as much as hers. Maybe −4.

    7. Extent   −2   +2

How much pain or pleasure is produced in other people's lives? Probably not much in either case. The woman's family, friends, and neighbors will probably be somewhat upset over the incident. Your mechanic, boss, and friends might be a little better off. Let's say −2 and +2.
    So what's the ethical "bottom line" here?

    TOTAL   −49   +23

According to Bentham's system, mugging the little old lady is decidedly wrong. The greater negative score shows that stealing will produce nearly twice as much unhappiness as pleasure. The theft is thus morally wrong. But notice that it's wrong because it would result in less overall pleasure than pain or unhappiness. Bentham isn't saying, "Stealing is wrong because it's the vicious and sinful violation of rights of ownership," but "Stealing is wrong because it produces more human pain than pleasure."

Example 2: To Party or Not to Party?

So far the calculus seems to hold, so let's try another example. On Tuesday, your best friend Marla, tells you she's having trouble understanding material in her philosophy course and asks if on Wednesday you'd help her study for a major exam she's having Thursday morning. (You happen to be a whiz in philosophy.) Kindhearted and devoted friend that you are, you promise to help. On your way to Marla's room Wednesday afternoon, you meet Tony who tells you that he's just heard about a great party being held that night at a college a couple of hours away. The word around campus is that the party can't miss; it's a guaranteed great time. Tony says he's going and offers you a ride. However, he's leaving within the hour. Which is the right thing to do—stay and help Marla, or go to the party with Tony?

Unless you're hopelessly selfish, you wouldn't have to think very long about this. Breaking a promise to help your best friend just to go off and have a good time is a rotten thing to do. How could an ordinary person in good conscience say that it's morally better to go party than to help your friend?

Let's see if Bentham's system gives us the same answer. I've given this example to all of my ethics classes over the last few years; the results have been remarkably consistent. Why not try it yourself first, before reading any farther?

	Party	**Help Friend**
1. Intensity		
2. Duration		
3. Certainty		
4. Propinquity		
5. Fecundity		
6. Purity		
7. Extent		

A typical tally looks something like this:

	Party	**Help Friend**
1. Intensity	+9	+3

Most of my students find parties much more enjoyable than helping friends study. So they figure that even with a guilty conscience they would still experience fairly intense pleasure at a good party.

2. Duration	+5	+3

The party rates higher here. The pleasure starts with the anticipation of a good time and the party would last longer than a study session.

3. Certainty	+7	+10

The odds of enjoying the party and feeling good about helping Marla are both pretty good, although the party's a shade more chancy. You've got to get there first, and it's possible that you won't have as great a time as you've been promised. The pleasure connected with keeping your promise is a sure thing. You'll feel good about yourself, Marla will be grateful, and your friendship will be strengthened.

4. Propinquity	+8	+8

How soon? The same in each case—tonight

5. Fecundity	+8	+5

The party's seen as probably leading to more pleasures in the future than tutoring will. The party—new friends, perhaps lovers, other parties; helping Marla—self-approval, feeling good about her success on the test, pleasures that will come from the friendship continuing.

6. Purity	−6	−1

The party lost on this score. My students think that it's pretty likely that in some ways they're going to feel worse after partying. About the only unhappiness that helping Marla would produce is feeling bad about missing out on a great time. However, the negative aftereffects of a wild party are considerable, ranging from feeling guilty about treating a friend that way to coping with a bad hangover.

The total to this point is +31 for the party and +28 for staying. Breaking your promise is slightly ahead. What does it look like when we add the seventh category (extent) and take account of the effects on other people? Well, your friend is surely going to be pretty unhappy if you go. But if you get around at the party and make sure at least a few people have a really good time, their positive (pleasurable) scores could really offset Marla's negative one. And that would make the party score clearly higher than the friend-helping score. At the very least, however, it looks like a real horse race.

So according to Jeremy Bentham's hedonistic calculus it's probably morally better to turn your back on Marla just to go off and have a really good time for yourself. But how could the outcome be close between keeping your promise to help your best friend versus blowing her off for a party? As I said above, however, these results are amazingly consistent. Even though 100 percent of the people in my classes say before using Bentham's system that the right thing to do is to stay and help Marla, 80 to 90 percent of them come up with scores like those above. Most of my students believe that the consequences of breaking the promise would produce more pleasure than keeping it would. And in a teleological or results-oriented approach, it's the amount of pleasure produced that counts in determining right and wrong.

I hope you're thinking that the problem here is with Bentham's system, and not with your original judgment that the better thing to do from an ethical standpoint is to help your friend. Remember, measuring the consequences of actions is more difficult than it first appears. So what's wrong with the calculus?

Example 3: Monday Night at the Coliseum

Let's take one more example and see if that will identify the trouble. Imagine that NBC wants to come up with a sure-fire way to compete against Monday Night Football. They try the following. They premiere a new two-hour show called "Monday Night at the Coliseum," originating from Los Angeles. Every week the names of two men will be drawn from postcards people have previously sent in volunteering (with full knowledge of the rules) to be part of a "contest." Their motivation? The winner will receive $2 million, the loser $1 million. The rules of the game? A few days before the broadcast, an NBC SWAT team will abduct these men, terrorize them, and beat them up. In the intervening days, they'll be subjected to all sorts of physical hardship, trials, and beatings. Of course, this is all being captured on video tape, and the highlights are shown during the first part of the show. Then the contestants are brought together before a packed audience at the Los Angeles Coliseum where they engage in hand-to-hand, no-holds-barred combat on live, nationwide TV. The winner is the man who beats the other unconscious. Then the loser is revived and tortured for the final fifteen minutes of the show. The torture is designed to cause him lots of pain, but no permanent physical damage.

Let's imagine that the show does really well in the ratings and 40 million Americans are riveted to their screens every Monday night, delighting in the suffering and travails of these two men. And this is not all that implausible. Violence has a big following in this country. Some people go to boxing matches or hockey games looking for it. Others find it in movies or television programs. Still others follow it on television newcasts or in the newspapers.

But what about the ethical side of this? Would it really be morally acceptable to put something like this on the air? Would it be morally better to leave the program on the air or cancel it? I hope you feel at least somewhat uneasy about saying that there's nothing wrong with showing graphic violence and torture on national television no matter how good the ratings. But let's turn to Bentham's ideas again and see what they tell us.

If Bentham's utilitarianism adopts as its basic standard "the greatest happiness of the greatest number," it's hard to see what could be wrong with "Monday Night at the Coliseum." What balance of pleasure over pain does the program produce? Millions of people get a great deal of pleasure at the expense of pain experienced by only two men. Even if two million people get outraged over the program and feel some kind of pain or unhappiness, it's still not close to the amount of pleasure the program produces. Besides, no one is dying, the contestants have volunteered, and they're generously rewarded. They can experience a lot of pleasure with the money they've gotten for their pains. Maybe both men end up experiencing more pleasure than pain. Could cancelling the show produce more pleasure than the tremendous amount continuing it does? How could we object?

But surely we'd have to object. A theory that approves of letting a few people suffer as long as it produces enough pleasure for the majority must have something wrong with it. Otherwise, we could justify anything from racial and sexual discrimination to forced labor to caste systems and slavery. As long as there's a greater balance of pleasure over pain in the end, nothing's wrong.

So what's the problem? Take a look back at the last two examples and compare the different pleasures involved. The one pits the pleasures you and others experience at a good party versus the pleasures of friendship. The other case weighs the pleasures of seeing someone else suffer against whatever pleasure would come from taking this off the air. But the *kind* of pleasure doesn't matter in the calculation, only the *amount.* Bentham's system doesn't distinguish between the pleasures involved. It doesn't matter what types of experiences produce the competing pleasures. All that matters is what produces the biggest amount.

In Bentham's mind, all pleasures are equal. As he puts it, "Pushpin is as good as poetry." "Pushpin" was a simpleminded game played in Bentham's day. Bentham thought that pleasure was pleasure; it didn't matter where it came from. Contemporary versions of his phrase would be something like "Having sex is as good as helping someone," or "Going to the party is as good as keeping a promise."

And that's precisely the problem, because all pleasures aren't equal. You may experience *more* pleasure going to the party, but is it really as good as the *kind* of pleasure you'll get from helping a friend? And do you think that the pleasure people get from watching two men inflict pain on each other is as good as other kinds of pleasure? Is the pleasure you experience from helping someone somehow better than the enjoyment you get from drinking yourself blind at a party or watching a fight at a hockey game? How do we distinguish among *types* of pleasure and still keep our approach strictly results-oriented?

JOHN STUART MILL AND QUALITY OF PLEASURE

The problem with Bentham's version of utilitarianism and his hedonistic calculus did not escape the notice of one of his younger contemporaries, John Stuart Mill (1806–1873). Bentham was a close friend of James Mill, John Stuart's father, and was the young man's godfather. James Mill was so strongly influenced by Bentham's ideas that he put his son through a rigorous and remarkable program of education aimed at producing the ideal defender of utilitarianism. Mill bought most of this, but after something like a "nervous breakdown" he began making important revisions in utilitarianism. Like his father and Bentham, John Stuart Mill was more interested in social reform than abstract theory.

The most important change Mill made in utilitarianism was concerning the *quality* of pleasures. Mill accepted the idea that the standard for evaluating actions is the amount of pleasure or happiness that is produced. He writes in his work entitled *Utilitarianism,* "The creed which accepts as the foundation of morals 'utility' or the 'greatest happiness principle' holds that actions are right in proportion as they tend to promote happiness; wrong as they tend to produce the reverse of happiness. By happiness is intended pleasure and the absence of pain; by unhappiness, pain and the privation of pleasure." However, Mill rejected Bentham's belief that all pleasures are equal. He insisted that we distinquish between a whole range of pleasures—some lower and some higher. He explains, "It is quite compatible with the principle of utility to recognize the fact that some kinds of pleasure are more desirable and more valuable than others. It would be absurd that, while in estimating all other things quality is considered as well as quantity, the estimation of pleasure should be supposed to depend on quantity alone." And once pleasures are separated into high and low quality, it makes sense in Mill's mind to claim that the better pleasures are so much better that a small amount of high quality pleasure outweighs a much larger amount of low quality pleasure.

Thus, Mill's ethical yardstick is similar to Bentham's in measuring only the pleasure that results from an action. But it's different since it identifies and measures *better* versus *worse* kinds of pleasure. It measures *quality* as well as *quantity*.

Evaluating Quality

We've seen that measuring the quantity of pleasure produced isn't too complicated. You analyze the end results of each option for everyone affected and tally up the total. But how do you determine the quality of a pleasure? It's not so obvious.

Maybe we should start with something easier than pleasure. How do you determine the quality of a record or tape? You listen to it. But you'll be able to judge it only if you know what to listen for—clarity, depth of sound, range of frequencies. Only if you've heard both low- and high-quality reproductions will you know the difference. Or what about judging the quality of clothing? Again, you have to know what to look for. Is the fabric free of flaws and runs? Is the lining good quality fabric and does it hang properly? Are the seams sewn so they won't unravel? If the cloth has a pattern to it, does the design match up properly on abutting pieces? Are the buttons sewn on securely? Or how about distinguishing between better and worse quality wine? You study the wine's body, bouquet, taste, and aftertaste. But you can make an accurate appraisal only if you have an "educated" palate.

In distinguishing differences in quality you rely on your *judgment,* a judgment that's been trained and developed through a fair amount of experience. Someone without experience with clothing probably wouldn't see differences that are so apparent to you. Your judgment may appear to be no more than your personal opinion to someone untutored in the area, but even though it's subjective, it isn't arbitrary. (He or she would probably recognize the factors that influenced your decision if you pointed them out.) Your judgment is based on real-life experience, and other people with similar knowledge and experience will more likely agree than disagree with your evaluation.

But notice that the process is getting less obvious. More intangibles are entering. When you make a judgment about the quality of something, it might be intuitive. You may look for specifics, but your judgment might also involve something intangible. How do you describe what goes into your judgment that one car has a better "feel" than another? Even though a judgment is *subjective* that doesn't make it arbitrary.

Let's return to the problem of judging between different kinds of pleasure. Mill approaches the problem like this:

> If I am asked what I mean by difference of quality in pleasures, or what makes one pleasure more valuable than another,...there is but one possible answer. Of two pleasures, if there be one to which all or almost all who have experience of both give a decided preference,...that is the more desirable pleasure. (Reprinted with permission of Macmillan Publishing Company from John Stuart Mill, *Utilitarianism,* Edited by Oskar Piest. Copyright ©1985, 1957 by Macmillan Publishing Company.)

So to separate low- and high-quality pleasures, we ask people who have the greatest amount of experience with both. And what will they tell us? Mill continues:

> Now it is an unquestionable fact that those who are equally acquainted with and equally capable of appreciating and enjoying both do give a most marked preference to the manner of existence which employs their *higher faculties.* Few human creatures would consent to be changed into any of the lower animals for a promise of the fullest allowance of a beast's pleasures; no *intelligent* human being would consent to be a fool, no instructed person would be an *ignoramus,* no person of feeling and conscience would be *selfish* and base, even though they should be persuaded that the fool, the dunce, or the rascal is better satisfied with his lot than they are with theirs.... Whoever supposes that this preference takes place at a sacrifice of happiness—that the superior being, in anything like equal circumstances, is not happier than the inferior—confounds the two very different ides of happiness and content. It is indisputable that the being whose capacities of enjoyment are low has the greatest chance of having them fully satisfied; and a highly endowed being will always feel that any happiness which he can look for, as the world is constituted, is imperfect. But he can learn to bear its imperfections, if they are at all bearable; and they will not make him envy the being who is indeed unconscious of the imperfections, but only because he feels not at all the good which those imperfections qualify. It is better to be a human being dissatisfied than a pig satisfied; better to be Socrates dissatisfied than a fool satisfied. And if the fool, or the pig, are of a different opinion, it is because they only know their own side of the question. The other party to the comparison knows both sides. (Ibid.)

Mill doesn't give us a system of differentiating between pleasures as much as he gives examples of higher and lower pleasures. The "higher" include: intelligence, mental pleasures, education, sensitivity to others, sense of morality, and health. Among the "lower" we find: stupidity, ignorance, selfishness, indolence, and physical pleasures—especially sensual indulgence. Mill suggests that the former are more characteristically human; the latter we share with other animals. (He would see the "Universal Declaration of Human Rights" as a list of what would produce "higher" pleasures.) And he finds the distinctly human or higher satisfactions so much more enjoyable that they far outweigh whatever greater amount of lower pleasures we give up to get them.

A stupid person may feel perfectly content with life because of what stupidity conceals about the world. But Mill believes that the individual would be better off if he or she became more aware of life, more intelligent, even though that would lead to some discontent. The pleasure associated with stupidity is low quality; that connected to intelligence is high quality. In the same way, somebody without a shred of sympathy, decency, or understanding for other people may get real pleasure from acting that way. However, Mill thinks that on balance she'll be happier if she acquires sensitivity and a conscience. Even though she'll experience a smaller amount of pleasure, it'll be higher quality and thus more satisfying.

Analyzing Pleasures over the Long Run

It's important to see that the higher moral, emotional, and intellectual pleasures are supposed to be better than the lower ones because they ultimately produce better results. And the word "ultimately" here is crucial because it shows that when you analyze the consequences of an action, you have to take the long view. We have to ask ourselves, "What produces the greatest good over the long term, not the short term?"

Mill was especially sensitive to the problem of long-term consequences and he illustrates it with an interesting example—lying. Let's say you're really in a bind and lying can get you out of it. You'd feel pleasure at the relief of being out of trouble, and who'd feel any pain? It isn't like stealing money from the little old lady—nobody's losing anything. Who's being hurt by a mere misstatement of fact? How could a results-oriented approach say that any practical harm could come from a lie? Definitely taking the long view, Mill says that truth telling is one of the most useful and necessary things for bringing about human happiness. Consequently, "Any, even unintentional, deviation from truth does that much toward weakening the trustworthiness of human assertion, which is not only the principal support of all present social well-being, but the insufficiency of which does more than any one thing that can be named to keep back civilization, virtue, everything on which human happiness on the largest scale depends." Except in an extreme case (where lying will save someone's life, for example), Mill sees lying as more harmful than beneficial over the long run.

Some of you may think that Mill's imagination is working overtime here, but take a moment to think about it. What are the practical, negative consequences of lying? How would you react to a friend who lies to you? For one thing, you'd probably think less of him or her as a friend. You'd be more cautious, less trusting, more protective of your own interests. You might suspect he or she is trying to manipulate you at times, and you'd be less generous than you otherwise would be. You might ultimately break off all contact. Or what are the consequences of you yourself lying? You'd probably distrust what others say to you (there's no reason to think they won't lie as well). If your lies work, you'd likely do it fairly often—which means you're sewing the seeds of distrust in others. You'd certainly develop an abusive, self-interested attitude toward others. Your behavior would probably encourage some people to do the same. Whichever way you look at it, the overall crop is cynicism, distrust, defensiveness, and selfishness. Now multiply that over an entire nation and throw in a couple hundred years for good measure. What do you get? A pretty grim place to live. No good will. People unwilling to believe or trust each other. Agreements enforced only by the threat of punishment. People looking out only for themselves. "Just one lie" won't produce all of this. But the widespread and growing practice of lying certainly could. And every lie produces consequences that make such a state of affairs more likely.

So John Stuart Mill gives us two important factors to take into account when we try to figure out the positive and negative consequences of actions—the *quality* of the pleasure produced and the *long-term effects*.

Stealing, Promise Breaking, and Television— a Reconsideration

In light of Mill's contribution, let's go back to the earlier examples and see if Mill in fact straightens out Bentham's system. Does he correct the problems of making decisions solely in terms of the quantity of pleasure produced?

The first case was the dilemma of whether or not to steal the money from the old woman. We saw that making a judgment simply on the amount of pleasure versus pain gave us an acceptable result, but these other factors can add something to the analysis. How does quality fit in? Surely Mill would see the pleasure you got from mugging Grandma to be low quality and far inferior to the pleasures associated with honesty. The long-term results? Your sense of respect for other people and their property would be weakened. You might not stop at one theft and the next time you might be willing to hurt someone. You might now tolerate or participate in a certain amount of what you take to be "innocent theft" where you work. Certainly none of these is a useful result.

Next we looked at the case of keeping your word to help a friend or going to a party. Bentham's hedonistic calculus didn't work well here. Does the notion of "quality of pleasure" help? This seems to be the crux of the matter to this example. The pleasures of going to the party may be longer, more intense, and may lead to more enjoyable times in the future than will helping your friend. But the satisfactions produced in both you and your friend by keeping your word, helping her out, and continuing the friendship have got to be worth more than the satisfactions you get from a drunken bash. This is definitely a case of a smaller amount of high-quality pleasure outweighing a larger amount of low-quality pleasure. (The other side of this is that your friend would probably be so deeply hurt by your going that her pain would surely outweigh any amount of enjoyment you'd be having. A large amount of low-quality pleasure can't offset a small amount of high-quality pain.) And the long-term consequences? You'd probably lose your friendship with Marla, and other friends would know you couldn't be trusted. You'd probably make Marla more distrustful of people in general. The long-term effects here would be much like the long-term consequences of lying. So when you take all of this into account, keeping your promise produces the most pleasure.

And what about "Monday Night at the Coliseum"? Bentham's version of utilitarianism was pretty defective here. It looked like it could easily conclude that the program produced more pleasure than pain. Here too, the concept of quality will help because we can see that the pleasure people get from watching someone else's pain would definitely rate as base enjoyment. Reveling in suffering is surely not one of the most noble or advanced human traits. And what about the long-range result of having such a program broadcast weekly on nationwide television? The program would only decrease the human sensitivity of its viewers. Pain and suffering—the real thing, not just representations of it—would become acceptable sources of entertainment. It would encourage people to think that as long as something makes money, it's O.K., no matter what the human cost. When we look at the program in this light, it should be obvious that a greater amount of high-quality human good would result from taking it off the air. At least a tremendous amount of extremely low-quality pleasure dependent on very high-quality human pain would be stopped.

CONCLUSION

Bentham and Mill give us a number of good ideas. First, utilitarianism or a results-oriented approach works from the standpoint that if we treat each other with decency and consideration, life will be better for everyone. There will be more pleasure in our lives. More importantly, however, Bentham and Mill give us a fairly useful way of identifying just how much good is produced by different actions. They tell us how to systematically study the results or consequences of different options to determine which one is morally better—that is, which one produces more human good or happiness.

Bentham explains how to arrive at a quantifiable measurement of pleasure and identifies several factors. Mill adds the concept of quality and illustrates how a complete analysis of consequences takes into account not just you and everyone else immediately affected, but the people who are affected both directly and indirectly in the long term. If you have the patience and imagination to produce such a thorough analysis, you'd have a solid body of data upon which to base a moral decision.

I want to emphasize, however, that imagination and judgment are important components in a results- or consequence-oriented approach to ethical analysis. (The trouble with Bentham was that he left out judgment.) You need to use your imagination to figure out all of the possible consequences of an action. If you have a variety of options, you have to speculate about what pleasures and pains will follow from each action. And you certainly need your imagination to figure out the long-term consequences of the options.

When we try to come up with a system that's as empirical and quantifiable as possible, we can't avoid dealing with a lot of intangible things— judgments about gradations of pleasure, possible outcomes, and future consequences. You can't avoid abstract thought and judgment in an ethical decision.

DISCUSSION QUESTIONS

1. Think about ways in your everyday life that you make decisions about whether or not to do something because of the consequences. Do you make some or all of your ethical decisions this way?

2. Mill writes, "It's better to be a human being dissatisfied than a pig satisfied; better to be Socrates dissatisfied than a fool satisfied." Do you agree? What if you could take a pill that would make you simpleminded, but content. You'd aspire to very little in your life, but you'd be happy with whatever you got. You'd no longer feel the anxiety that a normal, aware adult feels. In essence, you're getting the offer of a kind of childlike contentment. Would you take the pill? Why or why not?

3. Think about the example in this chapter about helping your friend versus going to a party. How would you decide what to do? Would

the question of what was *right* come to mind? If so, how would you solve it? What would you do if you were put in this position? Explain your reasons.

4. Analyze the following cases trying to decide what will produce "the greatest happiness." Use Bentham's seven categories (intensity, duration, certainty, propinquity, fecundity, purity, extent) and Mill's additional category of quality. Be sure your analysis looks at the long term.

   a. Your friends are all pretty active sexually, but you aren't. You were taught by your parents that sex before marriage is wrong, and up until now you never really questioned what your parents told you about right and wrong. However, your friends are basically decent people and sex doesn't seem to be doing them any harm, so you're feeling confused about whether there's really anything wrong with it. You're also beginning to feel some peer pressure because your friends tease you about being a virgin, and you're feeling increasingly uncomfortable with being different from the rest of them. There is a member of the group you like and who you know would really like to sleep with you. What are your options? What are the results of choosing each?

   b. You run a small engineering company of ten people. How well the business does depends a lot on how well you all work together. At this point everyone at the company is white and male. You need to hire someone new and your decision comes down to two people: the son of one of your engineers and a black woman who answered an advertisement you ran. You think that the woman is technically better (better education, more experience), but you're sure the guys aren't going to like it. You know them pretty well and you think they'd have a really hard time adjusting to the woman—which means that everyone's work will be affected. The current atmosphere in the company is "macho" and a lot of ethnic jokes get told. What are the consequences of hiring the man? What are the consequences of hiring the woman?

5. What are the consequences (short term and long term) of:
   a. smoking cigarettes?
   b. drinking alcohol?
   c. smoking marijuana?
   d. taking more serious drugs?

   How does your reading of the consequences make you think about the legality of each?

chapter 4

Measuring Actions

In the last chapter, you became familiar with the approach to ethics that says, "We determine how right or wrong an action is by finding out how much actual good or harm it produces." And we saw how Jeremy Bentham and John Stuart Mill define human good and harm (or human happiness and unhappiness) in terms of pleasure and pain. There are some problems with this approach if we talk about just the quantity of pleasure produced, but as long as we factor in the quality of the pleasures and pains and make sure we look at long-term as well as short-term consequences, this looks like a fairly reasonable system. It may take time, patience, research, and speculation. It may depend on certain assumptions. But you really can systematically analyze and measure the consequences of an action.

Nonetheless, a teleological or results-oriented approach has some important drawbacks. In theory, it's still possible to say that as long as the pain or unhappiness of some people is offset by the high quality pleasure it produces for others, there's nothing morally wrong going on. For example, what if the Nazis' medical experiments on Jewish prisoners had actually led to great discoveries that benefited the whole world? Would that have justified the forced experiments? Of course not!

Or take an example closer to home. Imagine that your search for a job after you graduate has come down to two possibilities. One job is with a fledging record company; the other is with a major corporation. The record company is small and financially precarious, but the people are young and interesting; and you're excited about seeing what the music world is like. The other company is large and financially strong with a lot of possibility for advancement; but it's pretty stodgy and conservative. Both companies have advantages and disadvantages, but you're yearning for a taste of "life in the fast lane," and you think that the record industry job is going to be glamorous. You and your mother don't see eye to eye on this, however. Your mother, who is a vice-president of an important corporation, warns you that the record company will be out of business in six months. Furthermore, she says that she knows you really well and has heard a lot about the music industry, and as a result she's sure that you'll actually hate the job.

Let's say you've left your mother's number with the two companies for when they want to contact you. Suppose the record company calls and asks your mother to have you get in touch with them; she assumes it's a job offer. What would you think if she deliberately didn't give you the message believing that she's doing this for your own good? She waits until the other company calls with an offer, and then says, "If I were you, I'd take this job because it's a good opportunity and it looks like your only option. After all, that record company never even called you after your last interview. They're obviously a sloppy, fly-by-night operation." So you take the job and it works out really well.

What do you think of what she did? Was it right? I've presented this case to lots of my students and virtually all of them think that what the mother did was wrong, even though she was motivated by love for you, and her judgment that you'd be happier at the corporation was probably right (given what she knew about you and the record industry.) That is, they think that even if her action produced good consequences, she still didn't have the right to interfere with your life. If you agree with this, you can see why a results-oriented approach is still missing something.

Furthermore, sometimes all of us say things like, "I don't care about the consequences. I've just got to do what's right and tell the truth," or "I don't care if I can get away with it. It's the principle of the thing. Cheating on an exam is simply wrong and I'm not going to do it." Sometimes we're more concerned with the deed we're thinking about doing, rather than the outcome. A results-oriented approach, then, can't be all there is to ethics.

AN ACT-ORIENTED (OR DEONTOLOGICAL) APPROACH

Recall from Chapter 2 that the U.N.'s "Universal Declaration of Human Rights" says not only that people need to live under certain material conditions, but also that we need to be treated in certain ways. Accordingly, the more we treat someone in line with these guidelines, the better his or her life will be. The more we depart from them, the worse it will be. If you and I aren't treated with simple fairness, equality, and respect, our lives are missing something and we won't feel really satisfied or content. Even if your mother the VP is right, how would you feel if you found out what she did?

This way of looking at things is the basis of the second major approach we find in philosophical ethics—determining the moral character of an action by examining the action *itself.* This approach says that human beings are special things, different from chairs, tables, rocks, trees, cows, and dogs. There's an *appropriate* way to treat people and an *inappropriate* way. Appropriate treatment will make someone's life happier or more fundamentally satisfying; inappropriate treatment will make it worse. And because of this connection with the notion of human happiness or human well-being, this way of looking at things then says that certain ways of treating people are worse—morally wrong—and others better—morally right—in and of themselves.

This type of ethical thinking says that whenever we deal with other human beings we have a duty or obligation to treat them in a particular way just because they're human. We have a duty to respect people's rights and dignity. Because of this, such theories are called **deontological,** a word that comes from the Greek word *deontos,* which means "duty." A deontological theory examines how we are obligated to treat other people, what duties we have to them just because they're fellow humans.

When an act-oriented or deontological theorist goes to measure or evaluate human behavior, he holds his ethical yardstick solely against the action itself. He doesn't even look at the results. He is looking for the intrinsic worth or value of an action. He is looking to discover how good an action is in and of itself.

This is very different from a results-oriented or teleological approach. In essence, a teleological thinker says that there's nothing right or wrong in any deed by itself; an action is made right or wrong by good or harm that's external or extrinsic to the act. A deontological thinker claims just the opposite. Actions are intrinsically right or wrong.

Judging Actions through Results

The easiest way of getting into "act-oriented" ethical theory might actually be to cheat a little and start with something that combines that approach with a results-oriented one. In a way, we could say that the reason an action is morally better or worse is that it produces so much high quality pleasure (or pain) that there's no way that any opposite results could offset it. It's like assigning a virtually infinite value to someone's pleasure or pain in a numerical calculation of the consequences.

Take the example of the forced medical experiments I mentioned at the beginning of this chapter, or recall from Chapter 2 the question of forcing the Andes villagers to move for their own good. We could say that freedom is such a high-quality commodity that no matter how much good is produced from coercion, it can't outweigh the extraordinarily high-quality harm that it depends on.

We might even put it this way. In discovering that some things have such high values, we've found a way to cut down the time of analyzing consequences. After all, if we can see from the outset that something like slavery is going to produce such incredibly high negative values, there's little point to bother going through the whole analysis to figure out the other consequences. It would be impossible for the good to outweigh the harm. Looking at the action first—especially in light of the quality of pleasure or pain involved—is at the very least a more efficient and economical use of time.

From this point of view, liberty, equality, fairness, justice, and various freedoms are so essential to human happiness that anything fostering them produces human good of an almost infinite value and anything preventing them results in pain of an almost infinite value. So there's much merit in analyzing the action itself.

Judging Actions

But even if that process makes sense, it isn't a purely act-oriented or deontological approach. It's still making a decision according to the good or harm some deed produces. An action is evaluated according to its extrinsic or instrumental value. And to someone with a teleological orientation, looking at the outcome might tempt us to cheat on an ethical decision because we can see what will advance our own interest. The worst version of this is giving in to the temptation of saying "the ends justify the means" (the results justify the actions). So it is best to examine nothing but the actions at stake.

In addition to the problem of peeking at the outcome, don't you think something would be really amiss if we sincerely believed that stealing things, enslaving people, manipulating or breaking promises to our friends are all O.K., as long as they produce enough pleasure or happiness? The process of resolving moral dilemmas in your own life, then, wouldn't be what most of us experience now. Instead, it would look like logical, dispassionate comparison shopping for a rock video, VCR, personal computer, or car (depending on the severity of the ethical problem). Don't we mix apples and oranges when we talk about, weigh, measure, and balance the joys and pains felt by our sisters and brothers as though they're nothing more than material commodities?

Or maybe it's more serious than mixing apples and oranges. Perhaps it doesn't even make sense to treat human good or harm as though it can be weighed and measured. Maybe human good is less tangible than that.

Immanuel Kant, a great German moral philosopher whose ideas we're going to look at shortly, wrote that "everything has either a price or a dignity. Whatever has a price can be replaced by something else as its equivalent; on the other hand, whatever is above all price, and therefore admits of no equivalent, has a dignity.... Skill and diligence in work have a market value; . . . but fidelity in promises and benevolence on principle. . . have intrinsic worth." This is ultimately the most basic idea of act-oriented or deontological ethics—the real stuff of human happiness can't be quantified, assigned a value, weighed, and measured. You can do that with material objects but not with people. Your car may have a price, but you don't. You have such intrinsic worth as a human being that it doesn't even make sense to assign a material value to you.

To a deontological thinker, trying to quantify what Mill calls the high quality pleasures is a project doomed to fail. It's trying to quantify the unquantifiable. It can't be done. It's like trying to figure out how important a mate, lover, or parent is to you by determining how much time, effort, and money he or she saves you. It's simply ridiculous to approach it that way.

MEASURING THE IMMEASURABLE— "HUMAN" BEHAVIOR

You may not be able to quantify the stuff of human happiness, but that doesn't mean you can't measure it. After all, measuring it is precisely what we try to do in an act-oriented approach. But what does an act-oriented ethical yardstick look like?

Remember that I said earlier that an act-oriented approach says that some actions are appropriate and others inappropriate. A fuller statement of this idea is that some actions are appropriate and others inappropriate for humans to do or experience. An act-oriented yardstick, then, measures how *human* some deed, policy, or treatment is. It's a standard that measures *humanity*, not pleasure, pain, happiness, or unhappiness. It tells us how much an action fits, is consistent with, or conforms to a standard of human behavior. So when we take an act-oriented approach, we look at how well an action measures up against a standard of what's appropriate for people to do or what's appropriate to be done to them. Another way of putting it is that we look to see whether an action goes with or against the grain of humanity. According to a deontological (act-oriented) thinker, actions that measure up or fit are morally right, and those that don't are morally wrong.

In many ways the most basic spirit of the "Universal Declaration of Human Rights" is deontological. (This is also true of our own country's Declaration of Independence with its claim that we all have inalienable rights to "life, liberty and the pursuit of happiness." In fact, the same could be said of any document or line of argument that talks about rights.) The Declaration says that people have rights to certain things just because they're human. Having these rights doesn't depend on their nationality, race, sex, age, or political and religious beliefs. They're entitled to these things simply because they're human. Actions that respect these rights conform to a basic concept of humanity. Those that violate these rights don't. The bottom line of the Declaration is: "People are entitled to these things, and that's all there is to it. If you violate people's rights, you're doing something morally wrong because you're violating a fundamental standard of 'humanity.' If you think it's morally justifiable not to respect people's rights, it's because you either don't understand or don't care about what it means to act like a human being or to treat another person appropriately."

But with this approach, we don't find out what's human by studying different societies and determining what is conventional behavior. That's the approach of sociologists and anthropologists. With a philosophical approach we look at how people *can* be rather than how most of us *are*. Or perhaps a better way of putting it is: we're talking about the best qualities and possibilities of humanity, the characteristics of people that are positive and uniquely human. So our standard may be more idealistic and theoretical than realistic and empirical.

A Digression—A Few Words about the Intangible

The obvious next question is, "So what's 'human' behavior and how do you recognize it?" Before taking that up I want to discuss the abstract or theoretical direction this discussion is taking.

One of the difficulties of act-oriented ethics is that it's based so much less than results-oriented ethics in the ordinary, tangible things of everyday life. A deontological approach seems to be more difficult both to explain and understand because it depends so much on abstractions. We all know what Bentham means when he talks about pleasure. However, "actions appropriate to a human being," "consistent with a standard of human behavior," or "characteristics that are positive and uniquely human" aren't quite as obvious. The vocabulary we must use in discussing act-oriented ethics is increasingly less tangible. With this approach, you're going to have to rely more on your mind—your intuition, insight, and judgment—than you did with results-oriented ethics.

Don't let this bother you, however, and don't think that an act-oriented approach to ethics will only amount to subjective nonsense. The tendency of the world we live in is to think, "If you can't see, smell, taste, touch, count, weigh, or measure it, it isn't important." It's understandable that lots of people have this attitude, because that's part of the legacy of empirical science and technology. But it's absolute rubbish.

The essence of many of the things you value greatly in life—love, trust, generosity, sincerity—elude our five senses. But they're certainly real and powerful. Try telling yourself when an important romance crashes that it doesn't really hurt and that you don't have something major to contend with. Or tell yourself it doesn't really matter when your best friend breaks a promise to help you study for an important exam and goes off to a party instead. "Civil rights," "right to life," and "human dignity" (not to mention "liberty" and "taxation without representation") are ultimately only intangible ideas, and yet look at their power in the "real" world.

The upshot of this is: Don't write something off just because it's intangible. If you work at it, you'll see these invisible things quite well. Only you'll be using your "mind's eye." In this chapter you're going to have to rely a lot on your mind or intuition to come to a solid understanding of act-oriented ethics. If you make the extra effort that's necessary, you'll acquire a new skill—seeing the invisible.

If the bad news about act-oriented ethics is that it's pretty abstract, the good news is that it's much more focused than a results-oriented approach. You don't have to look at consequences that'll come about in a particular situation, speculate about the different results from different options, or try to figure out long-term consequences. All you have to do is examine the action you're thinking about doing. And in some ways it's a whole lot easier to answer a question like "Is there anything intrinsically wrong about lying?" than "What are the short- and long-term consequences (measured in terms of high- versus low-quality pleasure) if I lie to my boyfriend tonight and tell him that I'm sick when I'm really going out with someone else?"

Back on Track— "Human" Behavior

After seeing that an act-oriented yardstick measures how *human* some deed, policy, or treatment is, the logical question is: "What's 'human' behavior?" Let's work up to that through some 'non-humans.'

Imagine that it's late September, and you're watching some squirrels gather nuts for the winter. One squirrel (named Rocky) takes a few acorns from another squirrel (named Apollo). Would you say that Rocky has "stolen" the nuts from Apollo? Is Rocky a "thief" who deserves to be arrested, tried, and convicted for this disgraceful and unethical behavior? Should he at least get a stern lecture on the importance of respecting others' property? Of course not! He's a squirrel; there's nothing "inappropriate" about his actions. What he does is perfectly "squirrellike." He's driven by instinct and his instinct tells him to take the nearest acorns he can find.

Or take another case from the animal world. If you have any cats at home, you know they establish a hierarchy or "pecking order." The strongest cat is top dog (so to speak). But as that cat gets older and weakens, the younger cats sense this and start pushing it around. Instead of showing sympathy and compassion, the stronger felines see their chance to advance in the hierarchy. "Survival of the fittest" and "rule by the strong" govern the world of nature. The animal kingdom regards illness and old age as weakness and treats them accordingly. But if you saw a young cat (named Aristotle) asserting itself against an old and infirm cat (Plato), would you feel justified in punishing it for acting "cruelly"? Would you swat Aristotle and say, "Aristotle! I'm surprised at you. You should know better than that. Nice cats don't do things like that."? Would you think that he had acted in a way that was morally reprehensible? Hardly. Cats have no choice in the matter. We may not enjoy seeing a strong, healthy cat inflict pain on one that's weak and dying, but we can't "blame" an animal that's only following its instincts.

But what if you saw your friend Holly steal a book from her sister Susan? Or what would your reaction be if you heard that your classmate Louis said to his sick father, "Sorry, Pops. I'm taking over the business." Most of us would be appalled. To say there's something inappropriate about such miserable behavior would be accurate, even if it's a colossal understatement. Although Holly and Louis did the same things as Rocky and Aristotle, we'd certainly judge them differently.

The reason we'd judge the people differently, of course, is that neither Rocky the squirrel nor Aristotle the cat knows any better nor has any choice in the matter. But humans are different because we have precisely what these animals lack. We freely choose our actions and we have the intelligence that lets us think about what we're doing. That's what makes us human. We aren't called "homo sapiens"—"thinking man"—for nothing. We think about our options and we choose on the basis of our conclusions. (I know there's a lot of debate about just how free we really are, but I'm not going to get into that in this handbook.)

So this is a foundation on which we can build a standard for human actions—choice and intelligence. Actions that foster these are closer to the standard. Deeds that interfere with them are further away. In the eyes of act-oriented ethics, the former are better.

CHOICE AND FREEDOM

Despite my trying to explain these ideas using such ordinary things as cats and squirrels, this whole discussion might be getting too abstract or theoretical. Let's try to ground what we have in reality before we continue.

Take the idea of choice, for example. How would you feel if your friend Wayne told his friend Carlos that you and Wayne would be glad to drive him to the airport—in your car? Or what if your parents told you they'd chosen someone for you to marry or selected your career for you? What would your reaction be to someone forcing you to do something against your will? I imagine that in each case you'd be pretty angry. Why? Most likely you think that other people don't have the right to do these things. You see yourself as being entitled to make decisions about your own life, and your basic freedom to do so is undermined in each instance.

That human beings are essentially free creatures is the most basic precept of an act-oriented approach to ethics. Forcing somebody to do something just doesn't square with choice or human freedom. So an act-oriented approach says that anything that doesn't agree with the idea of human freedom, anything that interferes with people choosing what to do, is morally wrong.

Many things don't square with personal freedom and autonomy, ranging from forcing someone at gunpoint, to subtle manipulation. Still, all these actions compromise somebody's freedom, and that's what makes them morally dubious. It doesn't make any difference if the results of the action are good ones. There's still something indefensible about what's going on. Even if you meet some fantastic person that you fall madly in love with when you're at the airport with Wayne and Carlos, it doesn't make what Wayne did right. He still interfered with your right to choose.

Look at smoking cigarettes or drinking alcohol. If we outlawed cigarettes and liquor in this country, we'd surely decrease the incidence of some diseases. But we'd be telling people what they may and may not do. We'd be taking a choice away from them and limiting their freedom. Even though we'd be banning alcohol and tobacco "for people's own good," an act-oriented thinker would probably object. He'd argue that there was something intrinsically wrong with what we were doing. No matter how much good is produced, what we're doing doesn't agree or harmonize with human freedom.

Now before you think that deontological theorists are anarchists, realize that an act-oriented thinker sees some realistic limitations on human freedom as justifiable. (For example, it's O.K. to violate the freedom of someone who's hurting someone else by stopping him or her.) Nonetheless, an act-oriented thinker would demand an explanation of why such limitations are justified. (After all, an act-oriented approach to ethics sees actions which compromise human freedom as being morally questionable—they conflict with an essential feature of humanity.) But a deontological thinker wouldn't accept a utilitarian justification—one that defended violations of freedom by saying that on balance they produced more good than harm. The argument would have to show that the rights of the innocent person are stronger than the attacker's.

Freedom, Morality, and Immanuel Kant

Personal freedom is so fundamental to an act-oriented approach to ethics that some philosophers have built entire moral theories on the idea. One such thinker is Immanuel Kant, one of the "all-time greats" in the history of western philosophy. Kant (1724–1804) lived before Mill, spending his entire life in the city of Königsberg in Prussia (modern-day Russia). Unlike Bentham and Mill, Kant was a professional academician. First a tutor and then a private lecturer, Kant eventually was appointed to a professorship at the University of Königsberg.

Kant is memorable for many reasons. One story has it that his life was so regular that the people of Königsberg set their watches as Kant passed by on his daily walk. More important is that Kant produced one of the most important systems of thought in philosophy's 2,000-year-old lifetime. Also noteworthy, however, is that Kant was fifty-seven when he started explaining this system in his *Critique of Pure Reason,* and that he turned out one extraordinary work after another for the next nine years.

Kant is particularly famous for his work in ethics. He is the most important act-oriented or deontological thinker in the history of philosophy. In his classic *Grounding for the Metaphysics of Morals,* he explains the basic moral principle or moral law against which we can measure our actions. Kant calls this principle the **categorical imperative**—a command (imperative) that holds with no exceptions or qualifications (categorically). In Kant's opinion, to find out how right or wrong an action is, all we have to do is to see if it conforms to or "obeys" the moral law. This is his ethical yardstick. Kant doesn't think he's really found anything new. He believes that we all actually know the difference between right and wrong. We just have trouble explaining the difference.

So what is this moral law? Kant arrived at several definitions, but the most important one for our purposes comes out of his understanding of human dignity and freedom. He writes, "Act in such a way that you treat humanity, whether in your own person or in the person of any other, always at the same time as an end and never simply as a means."

The key here is understanding what it means to treat someone as an "end" rather than a "means." Kant illustrates the moral law with four examples: suicide, a false promise, developing one's talents, and helping others in need. The second is the best example. Kant writes,

[A] man in need finds himself forced to borrow money. He knows well that he won't be able to repay it, but he sees also that he will not get any loan unless he firmly promises to repay it within a fixed time. He wants to make such a promise, but he still has conscience enough to ask himself whether it is not permissible and is contrary to duty to get out of difficulty in this way.... [He] will immediately see that he intends to make use of another man merely as a means to an end which the latter does not likewise hold. For the man whom I want to use for my own purposes by such a promise cannot possibly concur with my way of action toward him and hence cannot himself hold the end of this action. This conflict with the principle of duty to others becomes even clearer when instances of attacks on the freedom and property of others are considered. For then it becomes clear that a transgressor of the rights of men intends to make use of the persons of others merely as a means, without taking into consideration that, as rational beings, they should always be esteemed at the same time as ends, i.e., be esteemed only as beings who must themselves be able to hold the very same action as an end. (This and all quotes reprinted with permission of Hackett Publishing Company, Inc., from Immanuel Kant, *Grounding for the Metaphysics of Morals.* Copyright ©1981 by Hackett Publishing Company, Inc.)

The person making the false promise is using someone else simply as a means to his own end.

In Kant's mind, to treat someone as an "end" is to treat him with all of the respect due to a human being—or to treat her in a way that is appropriate, a way that "fits" the fact that I'm dealing with a human being. However, treating someone as an "end" means to Kant particularly that his freedom or her right to choose her own actions is respected. Treating someone as a "means" violates precisely this point. If I treat someone as a "means," I'm using him for *my* ends, not his. I don't care about what he wants. And I see her mainly as an object or a tool that I can use to get what I want. I impose my choice, my decision on someone else, whether he or she likes it or not.

Treating someone as a means to your own end takes an almost infinite number of shapes. It can range from crude physical threats and intimidation ("Go get this book from the library for me or I'll break your face!"), to skillful manipulation that someone isn't even aware of ("Gee boss, I'd really like to work with you on the Smith account. I know I could learn so much from your skill and experience. You'd be doing me a big favor.") to using love or sex to get someone to do something they don't want to do ("What do you mean 'dishonest'? If you really loved me you'd write this paper for me. And if you don't love me, I guess I can't go to bed with you anymore.").

But what these actions all have in common is that they don't respect the other person's freedom and dignity, their right to freely choose what they do. My manipulation short circuits somebody else's right to make a decision in the matter. I don't treat him or her as a free person whose wants and needs should be considered, but as an object to be used for my ends.

So Kant's "ethical yardstick" is pretty straightforward. An action "measures up" to the extent it respects personal freedom, choice and autonomy.

"HUMAN" BEHAVIOR—OTHER FACETS

A need for personal freedom and choice is one of the most obvious features of human beings. But many other qualities go into defining "humanity." What else can we add to our yardstick so that it can tell us which actions are appropriate and inappropriate?

Well, equality must be almost as important as freedom. How do you react to actions that treat people unequally for no good reason? What if you found out that you didn't get a job you were qualified for just because of your sex, race, or nationality? Wouldn't you say something like "That's not fair"? Many people believe that so-called "reverse discrimination" is morally wrong because it treats people differently according to their race or sex. And that isn't treating people equally. If we believe that people are all equal, actions that are consistent with or respect human equality are appropriate or fit the standard; arbitrary or discriminatory actions fall short.

And we could tick off a number of other things that most of us would agree should govern or be respected in our dealings with each other—dignity, respect, fairness, justice, privacy, and toleration. These are things that all of us as ordinary humans are entitled to experience. From the standpoint of an act-oriented approach to ethics, actions that don't respect these qualities don't agree with or fit a reasonable understanding of humanity. An act-oriented approach says it doesn't matter how much good would come from such actions. They're just in and of themselves inappropriate for humans to do or to experience. Accordingly, they're questionable from an ethical point of view.

INTELLIGENCE (REASON) AND ETHICS

There is one other feature of "humanity" that deserves a closer look—our ability to *think*. Biologists would probably argue that this is an even more basic characteristic of humanity than is freedom, thus the label *homo sapiens*. How does this fit into an act-oriented approach to ethics?

Recall that the conclusion reached from the examples of squirrels and cats was that there are two reasons we don't say animals "do wrong" or are morally responsible for their acts. They don't have a lot of choice in their actions (or maybe it would be better to say that the choices we see them making usually are heavily influenced by instinct). And they don't know any better. Since humans have precisely these things that animals lack, we hold ourselves morally responsible. This led me to say that choice and intelligence were a pretty good foundation on which to build a standard about human actions.

Asking whether or not an action is consistent with personal choice is easy to understand. We all know what "freedom of choice" means and most of us believe there's something wrong with being forced to do something against our will. So we can see the connection between freedom and ethics. But what about intelligence?

Intelligence connects with ethics in two ways. First, combining the idea of "intelligence" with "choice" makes the whole idea of morality possible in the first place. Also, like freedom, it's going to give us a standard we can use to evaluate how "human" different actions are.

Intelligence + Choice = Morality

The first way that intelligence relates to ethics is very basic and very important. Ethical judgments are possible only because of the combination of "intelligence" and "choice." The key here is the concept of moral responsibility.

When do you hold people fully responsible for their actions? First of all, when they freely choose what they do. You wouldn't blame a bank teller for handing money over to a robber at gunpoint or a friend who accidentally broke one of your records when he tripped over the dirty laundry you left lying on the floor. If somebody's action was either forced or accidental, we don't think of it as being really "theirs." He or she didn't "choose" to behave that way, and so we're willing to excuse them. It's the same with animals. We don't hold an animal "responsible" for its actions because it doesn't have the same power over its behavior that we have over ours.

But the difference between human and animal behavior is that we can *think* about what we do. We don't just act, we think and then act (or at least we should). And that's ultimately why we hold people responsible for what they do—because their intelligence gives them the power to choose how they'll behave. And that's where morality comes from. We think that it's all right to evaluate what people do because we believe they can choose how they act, that it's in their power to act better or worse. Remember, the main aim of ethics is to evaluate human behavior. But there'd be no purpose in evaluating actions if we couldn't do anything about them. Our rationality, our intelligence gives us the power to analyze and evaluate our actions, intentions, and the consequences of what we do. Without reason we would no more make ethical judgments about humans than about the creatures in the forest.*

Reason as a Standard of Action

The second way that intelligence connects with ethics is that intelligence or reason, like freedom, is going to give us a way to evaluate the ethical character of actions without reference to an act's consequences. (Intelligence is just another way to refer to our minds, our rational abilities. When we think about what we do, we use our **reason.** And because "reason" and "rational" are narrower and more specific terms, I'm going to use them instead of "intelligence." It'll make it easier to understand how this can provide us with a way to measure actions.)

Reason gives us a way to evaluate actions. But how does that work? What does it mean to say that reason is a standard for judging how "human" particular actions are? The key here is to understand reason in its narrowest sense—those mental operations governed by the rules of logic. The most basic rule of logic is simply that contradictions aren't allowed. If a friend asks "Are you going to the party tonight?" and you answer "I'm going and I'm not going," your friend will probably think you haven't fully recovered from the last bash. What you said doesn't make any sense. Both can't be true. You've contradicted yourself. It's like saying "Today is Tuesday" and "Today is not Tuesday."

Rationality is such a basic feature of humanity that saying someone is acting irrationally is a pretty obvious charge that they're not acting

---

*Before going on I want to clarify something. I've been talking about human nature and saying things like, "We're entitled to justice, fairness, and toleration because we're *human,*" and "Intelligence and a need for freedom are distinguishing *human* characteristics and make the idea of moral responsibility possible in the first place." Actually, I'm talking about *persons* not *humans.*

These concepts overlap, but there's a difference. To be "human" is to be a member of the biological category *homo sapiens.* However, as is clear from the abortion debate, it's not self-evident that being human is enough to make something a person. (The fetus is "human," but at best it's only a "potential person.") More is involved beyond human parentage—self-consciousness, the ability to choose, and so on. These other things are important in ethics.

Another way to look at this is that there's no reason why a *non-human* can't be a *person.* We see this in science fiction all the time. For example, Chewbacca, the Wookie in *Star Wars,* is clearly a *person,* although he is just as obviously not a *homo sapiens.* A better example for seeing the connection between being a person and ethics, however, is the movie *The Day of the Dolphin.* A marine biologist has trained a couple of dolphins, Alpha and Beta, to speak. Impressed by the intelligence and skill of the dolphins, a group of men kidnap the mammals and try to use them to assassinate the President. In the end, Alpha stops Beta from planting a bomb on the President's yacht. In addition, having figured out that the conspirators are evil, the dolphins then blow up their boat. Thus, these dolphins are clearly *persons* who are capable of moral deliberation and choice. Even though they're not *human,* they're *persons* and thus *moral agents.*

the way a mature, healthy human being usually acts. Especially from a philosophical point of view, we can say that behavior that's rational is more appropriate to humans. A contradiction is illogical and thus, strictly speaking, irrational. So there's something inappropriate about contradictions when we hold them up against our standard of humanity. (This doesn't mean that we don't all experience contradictory ideas, beliefs, and feelings. But it does mean that we [and the people around us] find the experience uncomfortable. If we don't resolve our opposing convictions or emotions, we feel tense or unsettled. The human spirit doesn't experience contradictions with a calm soul and peaceful mind.)

But what does all of this have to do with ethics? Well, remember that this is part of a discussion about evaluating actions without reference to their consequences. Let's take the example of lying. What's a lie? And why do most people think that there's something wrong with lying?

Let's go back to the example with your mother and say that you later find out that the record company left a message with her. You ask her and she denies it. Presuming that we all agree that lying about it only makes matters worse, what's wrong with the lie? You might first be tempted to say that the lie is deceptive, and that there's something inherently wrong with deception. But let's get even more narrow and technical. What's the most basic thing going on in this lie? Your mother is saying something false. And what does that mean but that her statement doesn't square with reality. That is, the most basic feature of a lie—and its essential flaw—is that it contains a contradiction between fact and statement. Lies cut against the grain of the mind's most basic requirement for logical consistency.

Strictly speaking, all lies are illogical, irrational and don't "fit" with the demands of human rationality.*

---

*I can hear some of you saying, "What does he mean, 'All lies are illogical, irrational, and don't fit some *human* standard?' Common sense tells you there are times when lying makes sense. How about lying to protect someone from getting hurt? Furthermore, lying is *very* human. People do it all the time."

Be sure that you understand what I mean. First, to say that a lie is defensible and that technically it's irrational and illogical are two different things. The latter means only that it violates the canons of logic. In some circumstances you might conclude that that's the *right* thing to do. But that's another issue.

Second, when we lie, a different part of us than the mind's need for logical consistency is in charge of our actions. Actually, our emotions are probably then in control. Think of the reasons we lie—fear, greed, love, hate. They're emotions. When we lie, those feelings are stronger than the mind's need for consistency. Now, the fact that people lie so much doesn't mean that, strictly speaking, lies are logical or rational. But it does show that (as psychologists have always known) people have an easy time doing things for irrational reasons. However, think of the character Spock in *Star Trek*. Spock is a Vulcan and acts according to reason, not emotion. And what's the result? *Vulcans can't lie!* Why not? They'd be saying something illogical. Vulcans may suppress their emotions more than humans do, but reason and logic are the same for both of us. And that's what I mean by saying that lying doesn't fit a *human* standard—the standard of human *reason*.

That's why we always feel that lying has to be justified (at least to ourselves). There's something about a lie that just doesn't sit right with a normally sensitive, mature human. In fact, notice that the unflattering connotation of speaking falsely remains in the phrase we use to refer to harmless, defensible deceptions—"white lies." So we can say from this point of view that the essential inconsistency of a lie is (technically speaking) unhuman because it violates the canons of logic which govern human reason. And an act-oriented approach to ethics asserts that an action is morally questionable to the extent that it's inconsistent with a standard of humanity.

The rules of reason also give us some insight into why an act-oriented approach would criticize things like discrimination and arbitrary behavior. If we take the idea that humans are essentially equal and that race or sex are irrelevant features on which to base decisions, a classic case of discrimination is nothing more than *logically inconsistent* and *contradictory* behavior. If I pay a woman $20,000 and a man $25,000 for the same job, I am treating two identical cases differently. There's no real difference between the people, so there's no good reason to treat them differently. My behavior is blatantly *inconsistent*. And since *consistency* is one of the first things called for by reason, an act-oriented approach would find discrimination morally dubious because it falls short on a standard of humanity. (When it comes down to it, most claims of unfairness boil down to something like this. Your "mind's eye" perceives the conflict, even if you don't articulate it that way to yourself. There's no acceptable reason for your biology professor to boost the final grade of his favorite student a little just to make it easier for her to get into medical school, for example. And so we react to the inconsistency by labeling it "unfair.")

Reason, Principles of Action, and Kant

Kant gave several different formulations of his moral law, the "categorical imperative." And one of them touches precisely on the point I'm trying to explain—evaluating an action by seeing how well it squares with the canons of reason. Let's take a look at that, and at one of Kant's examples.

Kant's version of the categorical imperative that depends most closely on the laws of reason is: "Act only according to that maxim whereby you can at the same time will that it should become a universal law." A **maxim** for Kant is like a policy statement or the principle governing our action. For example, your "maxim" when you bought this book was something like, "Whenever I need something from a store, I will pay for the article rather than steal it."

Kant believes that to evaluate the morality of an action, we should state a general principle that governs what we're doing and then see how acceptable that maxim or policy is according to simple laws of reason. And the best way to do this is to imagine what it would be like if everyone acted according to this principle. When Kant says that we should act according to "maxims that we can will to be universal laws," he means that nothing about the principle governing our act should be contradictory or inconsistent if we imagine everyone doing it. Picturing such a situation should reveal any problems. Rational laws—the laws of mathematics, logic or science—are supposed to hold universally, without exception. If we can't imagine everyone acting according to a maxim without any trouble, we've got problems. Our maxim doesn't measure up to the demands of reason.

The role of the rules of reason is evident when we look at one of Kant's examples—the false promise. Kant explains:

> The maxim of [the false promiser's] action would then be expressed as follows: when I believe myself to be in need of money, I will borrow money and promise to pay it back, although I know that I can never do so. Now this principle of self-love or personal advantage may perhaps be quite compatible with one's entire future welfare, but the question is now whether it is right. I then transform the requirement of self-love into a universal law and put the question thus: how would things stand if my maxim were to become a universal law? He then sees at once that such a maxim could never hold as a universal law of nature and be *consistent* with itself, but must necessarily be *self-contradictory*. For the universality of a law which says that anyone believing himself to be in difficulty could promise whatever he pleases with the intention of not keeping it *would make promising itself* and the end to be attained thereby *quite impossible*, inasmuch as no one would believe what was promised him but would merely laugh at all such utterances as being vain pretenses. [Emphasis added]

The point here is that a false promise breaks the laws of reason in a couple of ways. First, it's self-contradictory. My stated promise ("I will pay back the money") is flatly contradicted by my real intention ("I will *not* pay back the money"). Second, the reason my maxim can't hold up universally is that if we imagine everyone behaving this way, we're faced with so much inconsistency that promises would never exist. People would want things that are rationally inconsistent: they'd want to have their words believed, but they'd also want to be able to say one thing and do another. A promise depends on our behavior being consistent with our pledge. As soon as we stop presuming this consistency, promises themselves cease to exist. If everyone lived by the policy, "When it's to your advantage, say one thing and do another," only a fool would believe somebody's promise.

The second major connection between reason and morality, then, is that we can evaluate actions by asking how closely the actions themselves or the principles governing them follow the laws of reason, that is, things like consistency and the rules of logic. An act-oriented approach claims that the closer your actions fit the demands of rational consistency, the better. An act-oriented approach to ethics, then, says: "In evaluating how *human* certain actions are, we can ask not only, 'Does this act agree with certain human characteristics (freedom, equality, dignity, and so on)?' but also 'How does this act—its principles or intentions—fit when evaluated by a standard of rationality? Is it self-contradictory or inconsistent in any way?'"

"DOUBLE" DATING—AN EXAMPLE

Before we leave this approach to ethics (based on maxims, universal laws, and treating people as ends in themselves), we should see what this looks like in ordinary life. Take dating. Imagine that you're living on campus away from home. Before you left, you said to your high school sweetheart, "Don't worry. I love you. I'm not going to get involved with anyone else." And for a while you keep your word.

But then one day you meet this terrific guy/girl. You start spending time together, just to get to know one another better. And soon you're together a lot. But now you wonder if you're doing something wrong. You still feel as though you love your sweetheart back home, your new friend understands this, and you don't know if this new relationship will really amount to anything. But your new friend is attractive in a very different way from your love back home and comes from a different part of the country; you find all of this intriguing. You tell yourself that your sweetheart back home isn't being hurt by what you're doing and that you really aren't "getting involved" with this new person. You're just getting to know each other and having some fun together. But you also ask yourself if this isn't just a rationalization for cheating. You're honest enough to know that you wouldn't like it if the shoe were on the other foot.

So how do your actions measure up in this case? Well, first, are you failing to treat anyone as an "end in themselves"? The best test for this is to ask if everyone involved would consent to how they're being treated. Your love back home probably wouldn't. If you've got an understanding that you aren't going to be spending significant amounts of time with someone who may become your sweetheart's rival, he or she would likely think that you're breaking your word. Of course, the easiest way to find out is to ask. If your new relationship really isn't a threat to the old one, you might be able to get your sweetheart to consent to what you're doing. Or, if you realize that it actually is a competing relationship, you and your love back home might be able to work out a new understanding in which he or she is entitled to do the same thing you're now doing. On the other hand, not wanting to bring it up is a bad sign. You're probably afraid that you'll lose your love back home when you don't really know how you feel about your new friend. In this case, odds are that you're then *using* your sweetheart as a kind of safety net in case your new relationship doesn't work out. And that sounds like treating them "as a means only."

And how do your actions look against a strictly rational standard? First, what kind of maxims or policy statements can we come up with that describe your actions? What you told your love back home looks something like: "When I'm away from you, I won't do anything that will lead to my falling in love with someone else." Your recent behavior might be governed by: "When I meet someone attractive and interesting, I want to be able to get to know them and spend time with them." Is there any kind of flat contradiction or inconsistency here? Probably. Let's be realistic. Spending a lot of time with an attractive, interesting, and available person isn't going to bring you and your high school sweetheart closer. So you're probably doing the kind of thing you said you wouldn't do. It doesn't matter if you still love the person back home, that "what they don't know can't hurt them" or if your new relationship doesn't work out. What you're doing doesn't really square with what you said you'd do.

Can your maxims hold universally? What would the world be like if everyone acted according to them? If we all reserve the right to spend time with attractive people, despite any commitments we've made to others, we'd be crazy to believe any such promises. In practice, such a promise would amount to "I'll be true to you until someone more interesting comes along." And that's not much of a commitment. And a promise to be true no matter what keeps us from exploring interesting relationships with other potential lovers. The two maxims cancel each other out. You couldn't have a world in which both of them held.

Of course, you can have a world in which one or the other holds. People either stand by their word or there's no pretense of commitment and everyone runs the same risks. In short, if you really want your actions to measure up, you've got to give up either the new relationship or the exclusivity of the old one.

MEASURING ACTIONS—CLOSING WORDS AND A SURPRISING ADDITION

By now the idea of evaluating the moral character of actions without referring to consequences should make some sense. As I said before, an act-oriented or deontological thinker holds his ethical yardstick only against the actions in question and looks to see how well they measure up to a standard of humanity. How appropriate are the actions for humans to do or experience? How much do these actions fit, or agree with, a basic standard of humanity?

And what is a good standard of humanity? We looked in depth at two of the most important components—choice and rationality—and we saw how Immanuel Kant bases his conception of a moral law on them. And there are many more concepts to bear in mind: dignity, respect, fairness, justice, privacy, and toleration. Think about what is unique or most positive about humans and you've got your standard. As far as an act-oriented approach to philosophical ethics is concerned, the more an action conforms to such a standard, the more likely it is promoting or fostering human good or happiness, and so the better it is morally.

However, I want to conclude with a few words that you should find surprising. There is more that we can add to our standard or yardstick for evaluating actions—like compassion, understanding, sensitivity, and sympathy. These qualities are all decidedly emotional, but how could we exclude them if we're trying to describe a standard of what is best and most positive in humanity?

I said earlier that emotion doesn't play a large role in ethics, but that means to avoid using your feelings as a guide for your moral beliefs. It doesn't mean that positive and altruistic emotions can't come to play in analyzing some action, or that they don't tell us something that a strictly logical analysis misses.

Take the case of so-called "reverse discrimination." A strictly logical, act-oriented approach would probably reject using race or sex for any kind of decision because it's inconsistent with the idea of human equality. However, a sensitivity to the present, practical consequences of generations of discrimination against non-whites and women and to the frustration and indignity suffered by people who are in a competition which gives white men a head start might suggest that the "truly human" approach to this problem shouldn't be quite so cut and dry.

It's not easy in appraising the moral character of an action to shift from a strictly rationalistic viewpoint to one that is more all encompassing of human virtues. And it's difficult to know when to give one more weight than the other. But remember, an act-oriented approach deals a lot with intangibles and you have to use your intuition and judgment. The more you're self-consciously aware of trying to do this kind of juggling act, the better you get at it. It's like any skill—you improve with practice.

A POST SCRIPT — "NATURAL" VERSUS "UNNATURAL" ACTS

Before ending this chapter I'd like to add a word about an approach to evaluating the morality of actions that, strictly speaking, is deontological, but also significantly different from what you've learned. And that's the approach that says that acts are immoral by virtue of being "unnatural."

This way of appraising actions is deontological because it evaluates deeds solely in terms of their internal character. Actions are *intrinsically* right or wrong. People who think this way adopt "nature" as the standard by which they judge the intrinsic merit of actions. You find this style of thinking surfacing most frequently in discussions of sexual morality. Homosexuality and oral and anal sex are considered morally wrong by some people because these practices don't conform to the "natural" pattern of heterosexual intercourse. Similarly, the Roman Catholic Church bars artificial means of contraception because such devices or chemicals interfere with the "natural" reproductive function of the sexual organs.

On the other hand, this approach is different from what I've been talking about for two reasons. First, some people try to settle ethical disputes by using the idea of what's "natural" as an *authority*. And this is no more acceptable than using the authority of law, religion, individual opinion, or personal feelings.

Second, this perspective differs from that of philosophical ethics because the ultimate standard is what's natural, not what's conducive to human good. Clearly there should be a close connection between the two, but what happens in the world of biological forces and what's most positively and uniquely human aren't necessarily identical. It all comes down to how you understand "natural." Sexual intercourse for the sake of having children is obviously "natural" in a physical way, but making love solely for the sake of experiencing affection and communicating our caring for someone else is "natural" in terms of the emotional side of our beings. Homosexuality may not be "natural" in that most people are heterosexual, and homosexual sex won't produce children. But that homosexuals can and do exist shows that in another sense homosexuality must be "natural"—the workings of nature produce it. And in still another sense we all know that being able to exercise free choice in how we shape our private lives is also "natural" for human beings. Further, aggression may be "natural" to man in the sense that wars of conquest characterize millions of years of human history, but surely that doesn't make imperialistic aggression "good" and a positive trait for human beings. In short, talking about "natural" versus "unnatural" and trying to link "natural" and "ethical" is much more complicated than it first looks.

Though I can't go into such a large topic, I wanted to point out approaches to ethics that sometimes look philosophical, but aren't. In this instance, if you're confronted with someone who equates "natural" with "ethical," you're entitled to ask for an explanation of what *natural* means and how that links directly with the idea of human good.

CONCLUSION

An act-oriented (or deontological) approach to ethics, then, focuses exclusively on the *actions* we're evaluating, instead of the results or consequences. As is always the case in philosophical ethics, we use a *human* standard or yardstick to see if the deeds under question measure up. So the basic question in an act-oriented approach is simply: Is the action being scrutinized appropriate for human beings to do or experience?

But exactly how do we decide whether actions are morally acceptable without any reference to their consequences? The fact that moral responsibility proceeds from our ability to *know* what we're doing and to *choose* our actions led us to begin with the concept of *freedom*. Immanuel Kant gives us a basic moral principle which says that actions are morally defensible to the extent that they respect the freedom, dignity, and autonomy of people. And then working from the *rational* character of the human personality, we saw that Kant gives us another basic guideline to the effect that the principle of our action must be able to be applied universally and be free from internal contradictions and inconsistencies. If we add to our yardstick concepts like *justice, fairness, sympathy,* and *compassion,* we end up with a fairly good standard to use to determine the moral character of an *action itself.*

DISCUSSION QUESTIONS

1. Think about ways in your everyday life that you make decisions about whether or not to do something because of the actions themselves,

with little or no regard for the consequences. Do you make some or all of your ethical decisions this way?

2. Do you really think that some actions are intrinsically wrong, that is, that they're unethical no matter what the consequences? If so, what are they? Explain in commonsense terms why you think they're wrong.

3. Do you think there are times when it's justifiable to force people to do something for their own good? How about compulsory school attendance laws? What about outlawing tobacco?

4. Come up with your own description of how people should be treated "just because they're human beings."

5. Think about the dating example in this chapter. What would you do if you found yourself in this situation? How would you figure out the right thing to do?

6. Do you ever hear yourself saying that some actions are wrong because they're "unnatural" or "perverse"? What are they? What do you mean when you say that?

chapter 5

Doing Right— Why Bother?

The preceding chapters presented a general picture of the basics of philosophical ethics. We saw that ethics' overall aim is simply to evaluate how much an action fosters human good or happiness. We talked about what it means to use human good as an ethical yardstick, and looked at the two basic approaches to measuring human good—results-oriented *(teleological)* and action-oriented *(deontological)* methods. The former examines the consequences of actions and tries to find out how much human good they produce. The latter scrutinizes only the action itself, looking to see how well the deed fits or is appropriate to a basic standard of humanity.

There is, however, one more major topic that needs to be discussed, especially for the hardened skeptics. Some of you might be thinking, "This is all fine if you believe you should live your life doing what will make things better for other people, but only wimps think like that. The 'real' world can be pretty rough with everybody looking out just for themselves. You've got to take care of yourself first. Furthermore, sometimes you're probably going to have to do some unethical things to protect yourself or to succeed in life. So the bottom line is, 'What's in it for me?' Will worrying about ethics really make life any better for *me?*"

In fact, the ethical life promises rewards for everyone involved. Your friends and associates will obviously feel better about life and about you if you treat them decently. And they'll probably reciprocate, treating you the same way, which will make your life better. However, even if they don't, you'll still be better off. Because when it comes down to it, the phrase "virtue is its own reward" is actually true.

When I say that moral virtue is its own reward, you may think I'm going to defend that by appealing to some ethereal notion of "goodness" and say that moral excellence is just valuable in itself and that it's the most important thing you need in life. I might even say this is one of those things you can't really put into words and so there's no explanation possible beyond that. But then I would be asking you to adopt a belief for no good reason, and that is unphilosophical.

The best way to defend the idea that "virtue is its own reward" is to show the connections between being a good and decent person and the overall health, development, or maturity of the human personality. In short, the "good" person is healthier, more advanced, and more mature than the "evil" person. And who in his right mind would choose disease or illness over health?

This chapter will explore the connection between moral virtue and the healthy human personality. We'll begin with how it was discussed in ethics' earliest days in ancient Greece, but we'll also see that it's an important topic for some contemporary psychologists. And if you've never thought about things in this way, you will see that your own interests are on the line with every ethical decision you make and that ultimately the most important way to truly "look out for Number One" is to do the "right" thing as often as possible.

SOCRATES—THE HEALTH OF THE SOUL

The idea that one's own good is the ultimate justification for ethical behavior has been with us as long as ethics itself. Not surprisingly, the first recorded advocate of it is the ancient Greek thinker Socrates.

To understand Socrates' ideas, you have to know a little about his life. Socrates spent his adult life in Athens trying to prod his fellow Athenians into examining if they were living their lives properly. Socrates was the enemy of immorality, hypocrisy, ignorance, sham, and deceit, and he would regularly engage individual Athenians in philosophical dialogue to test their beliefs and encourage them to virtue. Not surprisingly, when you do this in public, (as everything important in Greek life was done), you're likely to offend some people. Without going into all the details, suffice it to say that after Athens lost a long war with its arch rival Sparta, some conservatives thought that Socrates' incessant questioning under-mined the traditions of Athens and contributed to her defeat. Socrates was indicted on the capital charges of impiety and corrupting the young, found guilty, and sentenced to death. His example will last forever as the classic case of the good man being executed by his fellows because his virtue and honesty underscore their own weaknesses. In short, Socrates did nothing that really deserved the death penalty.

The best example of Socrates' idea that moral goodness is like health comes in a discussion between Socrates and his friend Crito in which Crito is trying to persuade Socrates to break out of jail and escape execution. Crito can arrange it, but for Socrates the question isn't "Can we pull it off?" but "Is it *right*?" In trying to explain to Crito why acting ethically is the most important issue, Socrates says that doing wrong "will harm and corrupt that part of ourselves that is improved by just actions and destroyed by unjust actions."

Socrates' expression is pretty vague and unusual. Today we don't hear people talking about "that part of me that's improved by doing right and harmed by doing wrong." However, Socrates is actually referring to what we might call our "character" or perhaps our "personality." He claims that a central part of what makes us who we are is improved or destroyed depending on how morally justifiable our behavior is.

Socrates says it's like the body and health—only more important. We've got to do certain things if we want our bodies to be healthy, and if we ignore them we risk being in bad shape or getting sick. "And is life worth living with a body that is corrupted and in bad condition?" asks Socrates. "In no way," replies Crito. Making the connection with this "other part" of us, Socrates asks, "And is life worth living for us with that part of us corrupted that unjust action harms and just action benefits? Or do we think that part of us, whatever it is, that is concerned with justice and injustice, is inferior to the body?" Crito: "Not at all." Socrates: "Is it more valuable?" Crito: "Much more." (*The Trial and Death of Socrates*, translated by G. M. A. Grube [Indianapolis: Hackett Publishing Company, Inc., 1975], pp. 47–48.) So Socrates believes that moral excellence is necessary for the health of a part of us that's more important than our bodies—our character.

But what does this mean in commonsense terms? First of all, let's see what a "healthy" character looks like. People with healthy characters can accurately see the ethical aspects of what they're doing and can control those actions. People with healthy and mature personalities are sensitive enough to other people to know when they're thinking of doing something questionable, and they have full power to act the way they choose. This way of looking at things reveals that if you've got a strong, healthy character, you've got a pretty solid sense of right and wrong and can act according to it. An "unhealthy" or weak character lacks this **moral vision** and **strength of will.**

And this makes sense. Think of someone you admire as a really solid, decent person. I bet that part of what you admire is that individual's clear sense of right and wrong. When deciding what to do in his own life, he or she doesn't say, " I know I promised to help you, but I found something better to do. And since I'd expect you to do the same in my shoes, I really don't see anything wrong with it." There'd be no question that it's wrong to break a promise for such a paltry reason. And if that person gets angry at being treated unfairly or at someone else's being treated badly, you know that's the real reason. It's not sour grapes or blind loyalty to a friend. It's seeing that there's really something wrong going on.

Imagine someone you really trust or know you can count on in hard times. You're thinking of a really strong person who isn't swayed by the crowd but acts according to an inner commitment to right and wrong. If you trust this person with some secret, you're positive he or she will keep it. If you depend on this friend to do something important for you, it's because you know nothing will get in the way of keeping his or her word to you. If you take an unpopular stand on something, this person won't turn a cold shoulder to you, thinking that staying in the good graces of others is more important than sticking by you. There's real clarity of moral vision and strength of character here.

Now imagine someone just the opposite—someone undependable and without a conscience. Someone you wouldn't trust or confide in. Someone who would dump you in a minute for somebody more useful. This person might get more of what he or she wants than you do because of selfishness. But this is not "strength."

In fact, people like this are really weak. They're so weak that they can't really control what they do. They're led around by the nose by their insatiable desires—whether it be for money, sex, power, a good time, or popularity. And they have absolutely no moral vision. They can't see beyond their own needs. They know only how something affects them, not how it affects other people. Other people's interests just aren't part of their world. These people are morally blind. Strength and vision are at stake.

Health, Strength, and Moral Corruption

But what does Socrates mean when he says that our ability to differentiate between right and wrong and our capacity to be in full control of what we do is strengthened or weakened by how we act? What does it mean that the health of my character depends on whether or not I'm honest and treat other people fairly?

Let's go at it this way. Imagine that you have this friend who's basically a good and decent person, very bright and talented, but also really ambitious for money and power. He goes to work for a big company and after a few months is taken under the wing of an unscrupulous vice-president who sees your friend as a natural for the "fast track." The VP offers the following advice, "Look, kid, if you want to make it big, you play hard ball. You've got to be aggressive but politically savvy. You've got to use people and you'll have to step on people now and then to get ahead of them. Show no mercy. Be ruthless. Remember, you can't make an omelet without breaking some eggs. Every great city is built on the ruins of what came before it. You've got real talent and promise, but you're going to have to do some stuff your mother might not be too happy about. But then she didn't get to be a vice-president by thirty-five, did she? I'm just telling you the rules of the game. This is business, not Sunday School. Take my advice and you'll do fine."

Your friend has mixed feelings hearing this. He likes the part about getting to be a vice-president by thirty-five, but he's uncomfortable about the rest of it. He's basically idealistic and wants to believe that all you really need to do to succeed is to work hard. But if there are enough people like this VP around, hard work alone isn't enough to make it really big.

His dilemma intensifies when the VP approaches him saying, "I've got a problem I could use your help with. A month ago you got a report from Smith's department. I want you to call my assistant and complain that you haven't gotten it yet. Trust me. By the way, something may be opening up that I think you'd like." He's troubled by the request, because he's being asked to lie and he still is bothered about what the VP said in their last conversation. But let's say he figures that one lie can't hurt anybody that much while he decides how to handle things, and so he goes ahead and does it. When he learns, however, that the VP used the lie as a pretext to fire Smith, your friend feels very guilty. However, when he's offered Smith's job, the guilt starts to fade.

Now let's say that his ambition is so strong that he continues cooperating with his boss's conniving. He gets to be very good at it himself and he rises quickly in the company. What do you think he'll feel? Probably considerable pride at his accomplishments and abilities. And what about his initial reservations? I suspect that he'll dismiss them as childish, idealistic, and naive, wondering why he ever seriously thought that way. He'd probably see these ideas as weaknesses that would have held him back from reaching his true potential. He thinks that people who object to his tactics confuse morality with "vigorous gameplay." "The only people who cry 'Foul!' are those who lose," he says to himself. He sees nothing wrong with what he does. His opponents just look at it from the wrong perspective. He sees himself as having become stronger—having grown up and learned how to handle the real world.

But is his appraisal accurate? No. Is he stronger? No. Did he "overcome weaknesses"? No. What really happened? He's been corrupted! His initial reservations were accurate, but his actions since then did two things—they blinded and weakened him. They made him unable to understand the legitimacy of an ethical perspective any more. He sees less, not more. They took away his power to act from any principle more high minded than self-interest. He's grown weaker, not stronger. Instead of growing up, he's actually regressed to a more childish stage. After all, who is more self-centered than small children? And what's more childish than the attitude that "good" means "good for me"?

The most important point to see is that your friend changed because of what he did. He lost his awareness that there was something wrong about lying and manipulating people because he got used to conniving. The first time was difficult. The second time a little easier. But the more he did it, the less it bothered him. The more he did it, the more likely he'd do it again. The more he did it, the less he could see wrong with it.

His actions produced a kind of tunnel vision. The more his ambition governed his behavior, the less he could see any ethical considerations. When he looked at a situation, what jumped out was how he could advance his own interests. Other people's concerns became invisible. That's what I mean by saying that he became *blind*.

In the same way, the more his selfishness controlled his actions, the more he lost the power to act differently. We might say that the stronger his ambition became, the weaker he himself became. Ultimately, it just became second nature for him to act aggressively and selfishly. He stopped struggling and feeling guilty because he lost the power to resist. He lost the power to choose. Acting that way caused him to "forget" what he once knew about the importance of human, ethical matters, and it took away his ability to choose what was right over what would fulfill his ambitions.

The experience described in this imaginary story is actually fairly common. Whether you look at business, academics, politics, or any profession, it's not hard to find people who have forgotten their early idealism and now treat everyone around them as pawns to their own ends. They are probably very successful (although I'm certainly not saying that every successful person is like this) and they think they're doing the world a service. After all, people who have been corrupted are convinced that their point of view is much more accurate than all of those naive people who just remind them of their younger selves before they "saw the light."

Socrates, however, would say that no matter how successful they've become, they've gotten worse in the bargain. The part of them "that is strengthened by just actions and weakened by unjust ones" has been impaired. They've lost something. They've become more interested in themselves and less sensitive to others. They're more willing to do some unethical things. In fact, they probably can't tell the difference between right and wrong as well as before. (They're more likely to say, "Cheating's not wrong. Everyone does it." Or, "Double billing isn't dishonest. It's just the way you've got to do business to make a profit." Or, "Nobody really expects you to keep campaign promises anyway.") How could you say that someone who lost his conscience has become a better human being?

But the worst part of this is that Socrates believes that once you start being corrupted, you don't know what's happening. In fact, you think just the opposite—that you're getting stronger and wiser. That's why he thinks it's so important not to do something deliberately that you know is wrong. You'll start changing for the worse and not have any interest in stopping yourself. In a sense, you'll lose yourself.

This is why Socrates died. He didn't die to show the citizen's duty to the state or to testify to the sincerity of his beliefs. He died because he believed he had only two options—death of his body or corruption of his character (a kind of death of the core of his being)—and he thought that the latter was worse. Socrates believed for a variety of reasons that escaping from jail would harm innocent people. He knew that if he did something wrong, he'd stop being the person he was and become someone different—and worse. He was in a no-win situation. Death or corruption? No wonder he chose not to escape. Think about it. What would you do if you had to choose between dying or becoming someone who might deliberately hurt people without any regret?

SAINT AUGUSTINE AND THE "WAGES OF SIN"

I said earlier that I wasn't going to talk about religion and ethics. But sometimes ideas of religious thinkers fit in a philosophical discussion, that is, when they add something rational and secular. One of the great saints of the Christian church, Saint Augustine, was an incredibly perceptive student of the human personality, and thought a lot about sin and evil. He made some interesting remarks similar to Socrates' ideas about the effects of acting unethically.

Saint Augustine (Aurelius Augustinus) was born in northern Africa in 354 A.D. to a pagan father and Christian mother. He was raised as a Christian, although in keeping with the customs of the time, he was not baptized. As a young man he studied rhetoric at Carthage, where he rejected Christianity in favor of Manicheanism (which taught that the world is ruled by two principles: one good [light], and the other evil [darkness]). After teaching rhetoric in Carthage, Rome, and Milan, he abandoned Manicheanism, began studying neoplatonic philosophy, and was thereby led back to Christianity. After a powerful conversion experience he was baptized, returned to Africa, founded a religious community, and was subsequently ordained priest and then appointed Bishop of Hippo in 396. He carried out his duties as bishop for more than thirty years and wrote voluminously, frequently against what he saw as his time's heresies. Though he died in 430, his influence in Christian thought has been enormous. Called by Saint Jerome the "second founder" of Christianity, Augustine's ideas have affected virtually every branch of the religion.

Augustine has a special interest in sin and evil. He believed that before his conversion he had lead a terribly sinful life. And while we would surely judge him less harshly than he judged himself, Augustine pondered deeply on sin and its effects. Surprisingly, although Augustine's thinking takes a very different path from Socrates', he comes to a remarkably similar conclusion—in effect, that sin contains its own punishment.

As an orthodox Christian, Augustine believed that people would be rewarded or punished after death for how they lived their lives. At the same time, however, he talks about how doing evil leads us to be punished in the here and now. In his book, *On Free Choice of the Will,* Augustine describes the consequences of sin as follows:

> Lust dominates the mind, despoils it of the wealth of its virtue, and drags it, poor and needy, now this way and now that; now approving and even defending what is false as though it were true, now disapproving what it previously defended, and rushing on to other falsities; now refusing assent and fearing clear reasoning; now despairing of fully discovering the truth and clinging to the deep obscurities of stupidity; now struggling into the light of understanding and falling back again from weariness. Meanwhile the reign of lust rages tyrannically and distracts the life and whole spirit of man with many conflicting storms of terror, desire, anxiety, empty and false happiness, torture because of the loss of something that he used to love, eagerness to possess what he does not have, grievances for injuries received, and fires of vengeance. Wherever he turns, greed amasses, extravagance wastes, ambition entices, pride bloats, envy twists, sloth buries, obstinacy goads, submissiveness harasses, and all the other innumerable things that throng and busy themselves in the kingdom of lust. (Reprinted with permission of Macmillan Publishing Company from Saint Augustine, *On Free Choice of the Will,* translated by Anna S. Benjamin and L. H. Hackstaff. Copyright ©1985, 1964 by Macmillan Publishing Company.)

First of all, notice that Augustine is painting a picture of an unhappy, tortured, and unsatisfied life in *this* life. More importantly, however, is that all the details he gives come down to two things. Our minds don't work as well as before (defending what's false as though it were true), and we lose control over our own lives (our desires drag us now this way and now that).

Elsewhere in the same work, Augustine labels these two results of sin *ignorance* and *difficulty*. He writes, "It is an absolutely just punishment for sin that each man loses what he is unwilling to use rightly, when he could without any difficulty use it if he willed. Thus the man who does not act rightly although he knows what he ought to do, loses the power to know what is right; and whoever is unwilling to do right when he can, loses the power to do it when he wills to. In fact, two penalties—ignorance and difficulty—beset every sinful soul."

When you read Augustine's words you should be hearing echoes of Socrates. Augustine believes that the result in human beings of acting unethically is that we lose the power to tell the difference; we become ignorant of the difference. Similarly, by choosing what we know is wrong, we lose the power to choose rightly in the future; it becomes more difficult to do the right thing. Augustine doesn't claim that God is doing this to us. He describes it as a natural process that holds for all of us.

Saint Augustine and Socrates don't see eye to eye about religious beliefs, but they're unquestionably of the same mind about the effects of unethical behavior on the human personality. We lose something. It makes us worse.

ANOTHER TALE OF CORRUPTION—THE DARK SIDE OF "THE FORCE"

The ideas of Socrates and Augustine, although more than two thousand years old, even have counterparts today. We find them expressed in a number of places—not only in philosophy, but contemporary psychology and even science fiction movies.

For example, the idea that moral corruption involves losing both clear *moral vision* and *control* over our actions is actually a major theme in George Lucas' *Star Wars* saga. In the film, "the Force" is described as a fundamental power of the universe. But the Force has a "dark side." The reason that arch villain Darth Vader is evil is that he was taken over by the dark side of the Force, and Vader is intent on trying to lure his son, Luke Skywalker, to the dark side.

What is most relevant here is what's involved in being taken over by the dark side of the Force. Yoda, the Jedi master, warns Luke, "Anger, anger, fear, aggression! The dark side of the Force are they. . . . Beware, beware, beware of them. A heavy price is paid for the power they bring. . . .

The dark side beckons. But if once start you down the dark path, forever it will dominate your destiny. Consume you it will. . .as it did [Vader]."

And all of this is confirmed in the exchanges between Luke, Darth Vader, and the evil Emperor. When the young man tries to persuade Vader to give up the dark side, Vader answers, "You don't know the power of the dark side. I must obey my master [the Emperor]. . . . It's too late for me, Son." Taunting Luke, the Emperor says, "I can feel your anger. I am defenseless—take your weapon. Strike me down with all of your hatred, and your journey toward the dark side will be complete." And egging Luke on in his duel with Vader, the Emperor shouts, "Use your aggressive feelings, boy! Yes! Let the hate flow through you! Become one with it, let it nourish you!" (Reprinted with permission of Lucasfilm, Ltd. *Star Wars: The Empire Strikes Back.* Copyright ©1980 by Lucasfilm, Ltd. *Star Wars: Return of the Jedi.* Copyright ©1983 by Lucasfilm, Ltd.)

Although Luke is severely tempted to give in to his hatred and aggression, he successfully resists them and refuses to kill his father. However, had he given in to the hatred, he would have lost his ability to resist it any further or even to entertain that as an option. He would have become like Vader—enslaved to the evil Emperor. For all of his dark power, Darth Vader is ultimately subservient, not free. He does not have total control over his actions.

In short, this tale argues that we know in advance that if we do certain deeds and give in to particular feelings, our future perception and our ability to control our actions will be affected. If we give in to hostile feelings like anger and aggression, and if we start acting according to them and hurting other people, then in a sense we lose ourselves and get taken over by the dark side of the Force. The tale warns us before we take our first step in that direction that if we start down the path to the dark side of the Force, there will be no turning back. And there's no turning back because it won't occur to us that there'll be any reason to. It's as though we forget forever that there is a good side. If we have to choose what to do, we don't really see all of the options.

The idea that the dark side changes how we perceive the world and produces a kind of blindness might seem far fetched to you. But think about the "dark" side of the Force. Physiologically, what happens to your eyes when the light starts getting dim? When there's plenty of light around us, our visual images are processed through the retinal receptors called "cones." And a special feature of the cones is that they allow us to see colors. However, as it starts getting darker, our eyes work differently. Light is processed through the "rods." (When you go into a dark movie theater and can't see for a few minutes, your eyes are shifting over from the cones to the rods.) The rods are a lot like life—to get something we have to give something up. In this case, we get to see in dim light, but we lose good color vision. The colors are there, but because of the darkness, we can't see them. And if we lived on a planet where the light was very dim, colors would be only invisible, theoretical entities. To be taken over by the "dark" side of the Force is to enter a world where our perception of reality is altered as irrevocably as it would be if our sun became no brighter than the moon.

But the other reason there's no turning back once you start down the "dark path" is the *power* of the dark side. That is, even if we think about the good side of the Force every now and then, its power will seem insignificant to the power of the dark side.

This too might seem unlikely to you. But if so, it means only that you've never faced a situation where you started really giving in to your anger and aggressive impulses. You haven't experienced how your anger takes control of you and how you become someone else.

The "Dark" Side in Real Life

Without going into great detail about my private life, I will say that there was a stretch of time when I felt attacked, harassed, deceived, and taken advantage of by someone I'd trusted. The situation ended up in a lawsuit. My attorney was reasonable and sought a negotiated settlement; she claimed that the case shouldn't take more than a couple of weeks to settle. However, my opponent's lawyer was aggressive, hard nosed with a "win or die" approach to life. Through delays and technicalities he prolonged and expanded the agony—two weeks stretched into two years and the original lawsuit mushroomed into three. In the end, I decided to cut my losses and settle on terms I considered to be unfair. Why did I do such a seemingly self-defeating thing rather than "tough it out" to the end? Because the process and my reaction to it was changing who I was.

My "dark side" started getting control of me. Through all of this, I was frustrated and resentful that the whole matter couldn't be settled fairly and quickly. Furthermore, I offered reasonable compromises that took account of the fact that each of us had legitimate interests. But as each compromise was rejected, as the other side refused to put forward any positive solution, and as I saw that my opponent was doing little more than trying to dictate terms of surrender, my frustration grew and my resentment became anger. And since legal matters are long and involved and proceed according to their own pace, I had a lot of time to brood about what I felt as the unfairness and one-sidedness of the situation.

And as I brooded, my anger grew and began taking over. I started becoming obsessed with the situation and feeling really hostile toward my opponent. First I channeled that hostility into fantasies—initially relatively harmless ones, but later fairly destructive scenarios with my adversary as the target. But that wasn't enough. As the case was prolonged by the other side, and my further attempts at a compromise were rebuffed and my frustration and anger grew, I found that in my private moments I started seriously considering whether I could get away with a couple of things that were clearly aggressive and quite illegal, even if nonviolent. My aim was to get leverage with the other side and hope that they would then be willing to negotiate.

However, one day I saw what was happening. My anger and resentment had become the most powerful forces inside me—so strong that I was seriously considering doing things that violated some of my deeply held beliefs. My "dark" side was on the verge of getting the upper hand. In short, I was becoming someone else. My name might have remained the same, but I would have become a different person. In fact, the metamorphosis would have been so thorough that I'm sure even my appearance would have changed. If nothing else, my face would have had that closed and agitated look you see in angry people and my body language would have matched it.

Fortunately, before it was too late I saw who I was becoming and knew I didn't like that person. So I cut my losses and agreed to unreasonable terms. I lost a good deal of money in the process, but I preserved the core of who I am.

The point of this story is that I know first hand that the power of the "dark side" can overwhelm you. If it takes over, it will change you for the worse. Remember, Luke is told in *Star Wars* that his father, Anakin Skywalker, was killed by Darth Vader. And in a sense this is true. Anakin Skywalker and Darth Vader are two different people. The resemblances between them are purely superficial.

You're probably saying, "That's all very well a long time ago in a galaxy far, far away, but what does it have to do with ethics?" Well, it's a way of approaching this question of why any of us should bother doing what is morally right, or, to put it the other way, "Why shouldn't we simply do what will advance our own interests even if it involves some moral compromises?" And we find in the *Star Wars* saga essentially the same answer that we got from Socrates and Augustine. The Greek philosopher, the medieval Christian thinker, and George Lucas describe the same aspect of the human character. If we do things that produce human harm— if we are selfish, cruel, manipulative, or deceitful, or if we lie, cheat, or steal—then we change ourselves for the worse.

Although we may feel that we're being strong, powerful, and resourceful at asserting our own interests, in reality we're becoming weaker. We are losing capacities, abilities, and strengths rather than gaining them. We may think that we've learned how to lie effectively; in fact, we've lost both our ability to limit what we say to what's true, and any sense of why we should. It may feel like we have a new ability to manipulate and deceive; in reality, we've lost a capacity to really see other people's interests or a desire to respect them.

Don't be fooled by thinking that you may get more of what you want by cheating or stealing. That's only because you're using your wiles on people who trust you. In effect, you're "winning" not because you're playing better than other people but because you're playing by a different set of rules. (Think of it this way. Which team plays better basketball: one that can foul so skillfully as to get away with it most of the time or one that has a bunch of great shooters? Even if the "foulers" consistently beat the "shooters," would you say that they played basketball better?) Furthermore, you'd find out that you hadn't really become any stronger or more capable than other people if everyone else played by your rules. In fact, since being unethical is relatively easy, you'd probably find yourself up against some really stiff competition and you might not fare as well as you think you would.

Once we begin doing things that are ethically dubious, it gets harder to resist and we start losing a sense that there's anything questionable about what we do. We lose power or control over our actions and we start losing vision or contracting a kind of moral blindness. In short, if you ask "What's in it for me?," the response is "Whoever that *me* is."

ETHICS, MASLOW, AND SELF-ACTUALIZATION

As interesting as it may be to find this echo of ancient ethics in contemporary science fiction, it's more important to see that modern psychologists also suggest a connection between moral virtue and a healthy human personality. An excellent example of this is the work of the contemporary American psychologist, Abraham Maslow (1908–1970).

Maslow discusses a hierarchy of needs. He posits a series of five needs: physiological, safety, belongingness and love, esteem, and self-actualization. All of us have them. The lower in the hierarchy, the greater the needs' strength, potency, and priority. For instance, physiological and safety needs must be satisfied before worrying about meeting needs for love and esteem. The object of life is to fulfill them all—or at least as many of them as possible. Those who do are psychologically most happy and healthy.

What's of interest for our purposes, however, is the last need—self-actualization—because this is where we find Maslow talking about morality and the human character. In Maslow's theory, self-actualizers are the most healthy and most fully developed people you can find. They share the following characteristics. First, self-actualizers see life more accurately than the rest of us. (They are more objective and accurate in their judgments. Their perception is less distorted by their own fears, hopes or desires. And they are very perceptive about others.) Second, they have a clearer notion of right and wrong. (They can recognize good and bad fairly easily, and they choose the good consistently.) Third, an awareness of their own limitations produces a lack of arrogance and a sincere willingness to listen to and learn from others. Fourth, self-actualized people are committed to some work or cause they consider to be important. (They have a strong social interest and are concerned with finding solutions for society's problems.) Fifth, in a broad sense of the term, they are creative. Sixth, they are spontaneous, emotionally open, and courageous. Seventh, self-actualizers have healthy, well-integrated personalities. (There is a minimum of internal conflict.) Eighth, they are highly independent and private people, but at the same time enjoy others and form deep, healthy, and powerful relationships. Ninth, they are comfortable resisting popular opinion or the ideas of their culture when either goes against their own point of view. Tenth, self-actualizers generally accept a spiritual or mystical side of life. (They are not religious in the conventional sense, but Maslow claims that they accept the values taught by most great religions, "the transcendence of self, the fusion of the true, the good and the beautiful, contribution to others, wisdom, honesty, and naturalness, the transcendence of selfish and personal motivations, the giving up of 'lower' desires in favor of 'higher' ones, . . . the decrease of hostility, cruelty, and destructiveness and the increase of friendliness, kindness, etc.")*

The self-actualized person is really something. Maslow thinks that no more than 1 percent of the human population is self-actualized. Still, he believes that they represent the best that the human species can attain. Maslow calls self-actualization the "growing tip" of humanity.

Figure 2

Motivations and Gratifications of Self-Actualizing People, obtained through their work as well as in other ways. (These are in addition to basic-need gratifications.)

Delight in bringing about justice.

Delight in stopping cruelty and exploitation.

Fighting lies and untruths.

They love virtue to be rewarded.

They seem to like happy endings, good completions.

*A. H. Maslow, *Toward a Psychology of Being,* 2nd ed. (New York: Van Nostrand Reinhold Co., 1968); Frank G. Goble, *The Third Force* (New York: Washington Square Press, 1970).

They hate sin and evil to be rewarded, and they hate people to get away with it.

They are good punishers of evil.

They try to get things right, to clean up bad situations.

They enjoy doing good.

They like to reward and praise promise, talent, virtue, etc.

They avoid publicity, fame, glory, honors, popularity, celebrity, or at least do not seek it. It seems to be not awfully important one way or another.

They do not *need* to be loved by everyone.

They generally pick out their causes, which are apt to be few in number, rather than responding to advertising or to campaigns or to other people's exhortations.

They tend to enjoy peace, calm, quiet, pleasantness, etc., and they tend *not* to like turmoil, fighting, war, etc. (they are *not* generally fighters on every front), and they can enjoy themselves in the middle of a "war."

They also seem practical and shrewd and realistic about it, more often than impractical. They like to be effective and dislike being ineffectual.

Their fighting is not an excuse for hostility, paranoia, grandiosity, authority, rebellion, etc., but is for the sake of setting things right. It is problem-centered.

They manage somehow simultaneously to love the world as it is and to try to improve it.

In all cases there was some hope that people and nature and society could be improved.

In all cases it was as if they could see both good and evil realistically.

They respond to the challenge in a job.

A chance to improve the situation or the operation is a big reward. They enjoy improving things.

Observations generally indicate great pleasure in their children and in helping them grow into good adults.

They do not need or seek for or even enjoy very much flattery, applause, popularity, status, prestige, money, honors, etc.

Expressions of gratitude, or at least of awareness of their good fortune, are common.

They have a sense of *noblesse oblige.* It is the duty of the superior, of the one who sees and knows, to be patient and tolerant, as with children.

They tend to be attracted by mystery, unsolved problems, by the unknown and the challenging, rather than to be frightened by them.

They enjoy bringing about law and order in the chaotic, messy or confused, or dirty and unclean situation.

They hate (and fight) corruption, cruelty, malice, dishonesty, pomposity, phoniness, and faking.

They try to free themselves from illusions, to look at the facts courageously, to take away the blindfold.

They feel it is a pity for talent to be wasted.

They do not do mean things, and they respond with anger when other people do mean things.

They tend to feel that every person should have an opportunity to develop to his highest potential, to have a fair chance, to have equal opportunity.

They like doing things well, "doing a good job," "to do well what needs doing." This means "bringing about good workmanship."

One advantage of being a boss is the right to give away the corporation's money, to choose which good causes to help. They enjoy giving their own money away to causes they consider important, good, worthwhile, etc. Pleasure in philanthropy.

They enjoy watching and helping the self-actualizing of others, especially of the young.

They enjoy watching happiness and helping to bring it about.

They get great pleasure from knowing admirable people (courageous, honest, effective, "straight," "big," creative, saintly, etc.) "My work brings me in contact with many fine people."

They enjoy taking on responsibilities (that they can handle well), and certainly don't fear or evade their responsibilities. They respond to responsibility.

They uniformly consider their work to be worthwhile, important, even essential.

They enjoy greater efficiency, making an operation more neat, compact, simpler, faster, less expensive, turning out a better product, doing with less parts, a smaller number of operations, less clumsiness, less effort, more foolproof, safer, more "elegant," less laborious.

(From *The Farther Reaches of Human Nature* by Abraham Maslow. Copyright ©1971 by Bertha G. Maslow. Reprinted by permission of Viking, Penguin Inc.)

What's important about Maslow's concept of the self-actualized person for our purposes is that moral virtue is such a conspicuous part of it. Self-actualized people have a clear sense of right and wrong. They are highly principled and motivated by social good. Furthermore, Maslow claims that they tend to agree about the matters of right and wrong. In fact, he suggests that because of this argument, their "value judgments" seem to be more objective than subjective. He writes that "at least in the group I studied they tended to agree about what was right and wrong, as if they were perceiving something real and extrahuman rather than comparing tastes that might be relative to the individual person."

Maslow suggests that this agreement on values actually proceeds from their superior ability to perceive reality. The difference between them and us is that they see the world more accurately and therefore know more about what is appropriate to do. Simply stated, because of what they know about the world (what *is* the case), they know what things ought to be done. Malsow observes, "This is where knowledge brings certainty of decision, action, choice and what to do, and therefore, strength of arm. This is very much like the situation with a surgeon or dentist. The surgeon opening up the abdomen and finding an inflamed appendix knows that it had better be cut out because if it bursts it will kill the person. This is an example of truth dictating what must be done, of the *is* dictating the *ought.*" Elsewhere he puts it this way,

> [This kind of] cognition can lead to moral sureness and decisiveness, in just about the same sense that the high IQ can lead to a clear perception of a complicated set of facts, or in about the same sense that a constitutionally sensitive aesthetic perceiver tends to see very clearly what color-blind people cannot see or what other people do not see. It makes no difference that one million color-blind people cannot see that the rug is colored green. They may think it is colored gray, but this will make no difference to the person who clearly, vividly, and unmistakably perceives the truth of the matter. . . . I believe that the average person can then be described as is-perceptive but ought-blind. The healthy person is more ought-perceptive.

Self-Actualizers: Moral Vision and the Objectivity of Ethics

Maslow gives us some important ideas. First he says that all of the things that we consider to be a part of someone with a strong moral character are characteristics of the healthy human personality. (The other side of this is obviously that people who regularly manipulate others, cheat, or otherwise increase human harm are doing things that are in some sense "unhealthy," or at least signs of a weak or less developed personality.) Next he says that these people tend to agree on "value judgments." And then he suggests that for self-actualized individuals, these value judgments are objective and based on how well they can see the world. Their sense of right and wrong results from how well they perceive reality.

Let's take the idea about morality and the healthy personality first because this is virtually identical with Socrates' ideas. Both men think that ethical behavior is consistent with the strong, healthy human personality. And both imply that unethical behavior is unhealthy. It's especially significant that Maslow uses the concept of health because this isn't something a practicing psychologist of his training would use lightly. By using this term, then, he's offering an objective basis to his arguments. Also see that Maslow's theory suggests that ethically appropriate behavior benefits and that unethical behavior harms the doer. The ultimate justification of morality, then, is the well-being of the individual involved. All of which means that over the long haul, it makes about as much sense to be habitually self-interested and manipulative as it does to get addicted to heroin.

Let's consider Maslow's idea that the self-actualizers tend to agree on their judgments about right and wrong, and that this is the result of their superior perception of reality. Maslow's color blindness analogy that I just quoted is fascinating, especially when you consider it's made by a psychologist who was studying self-actualizers for years. The most developed humans, he claims, can probably "see" and identify the ethical dimensions and implications of actions or policies as clearly as you and I can see and identify the colors in flowers.

But what is it that these people see as they look at reality? What does Maslow mean when he says that self-actualized people are "ought-perceptive"? No doubt, this includes everything we've been talking about in the preceding four chapters. Self-actualizers see the intangible human dimension of problems. They see the human cost of different actions or policies. They see the consequences of actions (how much and what kind of human good or harm is produced by different deeds.) They see the ethical character of actions themselves (how appropriate certain actions are for humans to do or experience, how well particular actions "fit" with human nature). And on the basis of what these people see about the world, they make judgments about what *ought* to happen. Furthermore, as a group, they generally agree. That is, their perception leads them to roughly the same conclusions about what will maximize human good and minimize human harm.

One of the most important implications of this is that ethical judgments are basically objective. Maslow suggests that when self-actualized humans make ethical judgments, they use a standard of human good that is universal, not relative to either an individual or culture. And this is something that you should think long and hard about if you believe that ethical judgments are all relative, subjective, or arbitrary.

When it comes down to it, Maslow doesn't really offer us ideas that we don't already find in Socrates. The two thinkers state things differently, but both assert an ultimate connection between moral goodness and a healthy, advanced, and well-developed human personality. What Maslow does that Socrates doesn't do, however, is to base his findings on research. If you don't like what Socrates says, you can dismiss it with a remark like "What does he know about the real world, he's just a philosopher spinning out his own ideas." But you can't do that with Maslow's work. There may be ways of questioning it, but you can't argue that he's got a body of research which convinces him that there is this ethical dimension to the self-actualized human being.

On the basis of all of this, it is pointless to argue that ethics is a totally personal, subjective, or relative matter or, worse still, that it's a sign of strength to be able to be firmly committed to advance your own interest no matter whom you step on. According to Maslow, that would be like a color-blind person trying to convince the rest of us that colors are figments of our imagination, or that his way of seeing the world is superior than ours because it doesn't have all of the distractions we have. And that should really give you pause. (By the way, Maslow also says that self-actualizers enjoy sex more than average people do. So if a healthy, advanced personality isn't enough to make you take ethics seriously, maybe a good sex life is.)

MORE PSYCHOLOGICAL BACKING—KOHLBERG AND GILLIGAN ON MORAL DEVELOPMENT

Maslow isn't the only psychologist to propound the idea that a sense of morality is a fixture of the healthy human personality. In contemporary American psychology, interest is rapidly growing in what's come to be called **moral development theory.** What's really interesting about moral development theorists, however, is that they claim to be able to identify the characteristics of a fully developed moral sense and to chart the stages that people go through in achieving it. In fact, one of the most intriguing aspects of moral development theory is that there may be fundamental differences in the way men and women perceive moral choices and make ethical decisions. I'm going to conclude this chapter with a brief look at the work of the two most important American psychologists in this field: Lawrence Kohlberg and Carol Gilligan, both of Harvard University.

Lawrence Kohlberg: Stages and Justice

Inspired by Swiss psychologist Jean Piaget's attempt to apply a structural approach to moral development, Lawrence Kohlberg worked in this field for decades. Kohlberg claims that there are three levels of moral reasoning (**preconventional, conventional,** and **postconventional**) and that each level has two stages. Accordingly, we can identify what level of moral development someone is at. We can see how far along someone's come and how far they still have to go.

At the *preconventional* level, good and bad is understood in terms of reward, punishment, and power. (Children from ages four to ten are usually at this level.) In Stage 1, all that counts is power. "Good" is what the person with the most power says is "good." Stage 2 advances on this slightly, with "good" being seen as something that will bring about some benefit to the individual.

People at the *conventional* level take as their moral standard the expectations and rules of their family or society. At Stage 3, "good" behavior is seen as pleasing or helping others or at least trying to. At Stage 4 social order is most important; doing one's duty, respecting authority, and maintaining the status quo are seen as good in themselves.

At the *postconventional* level, people make moral decisions according to autonomous moral principles. Stage 5 has a social contract and utilitarian orientation; right and wrong depend on free agreement or standards adopted by the whole society. At Stage 6, right and wrong are determined according to individually chosen universal ethical principles— justice, fairness, equality and the like, but primarily justice.

Thus, Kohlberg claims that people at each stage act for quite different reasons. For example, he shows how individuals can differ when it comes to "obeying rules":

> The six stages look like this: 1. Obey rules to avoid punishment; 2. Conform to obtain rewards, have favors returned, and so on; 3. Conform to avoid disapproval, dislike by others; 4. Conform to avoid censure by legitimate authorities and resultant guilt; 5. Conform to maintain the respect of the impartial spectator judging in terms of community welfare; 6. Conform to avoid self-condemnation. (Lawrence Kohlberg, "The Child as Moral Philosopher," in *Moral Education,* edited by Barry I. Chazan and Jonas F. Soltis [New York: Teachers College Press, 1973], pp. 135–136.)

According to Kohlberg, the most fully developed or "advanced" way to behave is very Kantian—assessing our behavior according to universal, abstract moral principles. This is very "act-oriented" (deontological). If you're thinking of stealing something from your college bookstore, Kohlberg would say that the best answer you could give would be, "Stealing violates basic moral principles which I have a deep allegiance to." (The worst would be, "I'm not going to steal because I'll probably be caught and punished.")

Human moral development, according to Kohlberg, means going through these six stages in this order. Full development means getting at least to Stage 5. Furthermore, Kohlberg claims that his research shows that these stages are valid across cultures. There may be surface differences in the way different cultures manifest each stage and people may go through them at different rates in different cultures, but the sequence itself holds firm.

Echoing Maslow, then, Kohlberg contends that making decisions according to universal principles of justice isn't just *different* but *better* than deciding according to self-interest or considerations of power. A commitment to ethical principles is characteristic of full human development. Preconventional and conventional moral reasoning are in a very real sense more or less primitive.

Carol Gilligan: The Ethic of Care

Carol Gilligan basically agrees with Kohlberg that there are specific stages of moral development that characterize the healthy, fully developed human personality. However, she takes sharp issue with the stages themselves and introduces the fascinating thesis that they differ between men and women.*

Taking her cue from the fact that Kohlberg's initial studies did not include any women or girls, Gilligan saw that women generally fared badly when their moral reasoning was charted by Kohlberg's system. Women's responses to cases both real and hypothetical generally focused on how much actual harm or good was done. And Kohlberg's system sees this as a "conventional" response, indicating that the woman was at Stage 3 or 4.

As a result, Gilligan posited that most women actually employ a quite different ethical approach than the one most men use. This led her to claim that there are two distinct ethics at work—an ethic of *justice* (measured by Kohlberg and used by most men) and an ethic of *care* (used by most women).

The **ethic of care** focuses on our responsibility to help others and minimize actual harm. This account of moral development also suggests

---

*Carol Gilligan, *In a Different Voice: Psychological Theory and Women's Development* (Cambridge: Harvard University Press, 1982).

stages or perspectives, but different ones from Kohlberg's. The first stage is characterized by caring only for the self in order to ensure survival. This is followed by a transitional phase in which this attitude is criticized as selfish and in which the individual begins to see connections between the self and others. The second stage then is characterized by a sense of responsibility, and "good" is equated with caring for others. Devotion to others' interests to the exclusion of one's own ultimately takes its toll, however. This leads to a second transition in which the tensions between the responsibility to care for others and the need to have one's own needs met are resolved. The third and final stage is then defined by the acceptance of the principle of care as an individually chosen universal ethical principle which condemns exploitation and hurt in the lives of others and ourselves.

As Gilligan explains it, the ethic of care rests on the idea that no one should be hurt. This differs from Kohlberg's **ethic of justice** which is built on the idea that everyone should be treated the same. The central moral command of the ethic of care is to "discern and alleviate the 'real and recognizable trouble' of this world." By contrast, the prime moral imperative of the ethic of justice is "to respect the rights of others and thus to protect from interference the rights to life and self-fulfillment." Gilligan calls the ethic of justice a **morality of rights** and the ethic of care a **morality of responsibility.**

Equality and Equity

Gilligan sees **fairness** and **equality** as the main ideas undergirding the former, whereas the latter's premise is a concept of **equity.** Fairness and equality call for strict impartiality and blind justice. The world of law is big on equality. Equity, however, isn't blind at all. It looks very carefully at the particulars of a situation and allows for people to be treated differently if they have different needs. People who make exceptions to policies because of extenuating circumstances decide according to a principle of equity.

Take this example. Your teacher in this course announces a firm policy about missing exams. If you don't show up, you may take a make-up exam, but your grade will be lowered a full step. Her reason is that everyone in the class is in the same boat with about the same demands on their time. If you miss the exam, even if you're sick, you're ending up with more time at your disposal than the rest of the class. Since you have more time, you should be more familiar with the material and should do better on the test than your classmates. The penalty is just a way to make things fair and equal for everyone.

Now imagine that three people miss the next exam. Christy over-slept, Jennifer came down with the flu, and Rehan had spent the entire night before the test and most of the morning talking to his friend Mark who was so despondent that he said he'd even thought of killing himself. This was the first time in Rehan's life someone had told him that. He had no idea Mark was so depressed because Mark kept all of his feelings to himself. Rehan was stunned by the experience and totally at a loss about what to do. He's trying to get Mark to go to a psychologist, but Mark is resisting. Rehan was too upset to think, never mind take an exam.

Strictly speaking, according to a principle of justice, fairness, and equality, Rehan should be penalized on the make-up exam. The rule was clear, he understood and broke it. If his professor lets him off the hook, isn't that unfair to the rest of the class? If she doesn't penalize him and still penalizes the other two students who missed the test, wouldn't she be really unfair to them? All three students did the same thing. Shouldn't all be treated equally?

Yet maybe such a legalistic approach isn't appropriate. And this is where equity comes in. A principle of equity lets you look at the cirumstances and in effect treat similar cases differently. We might say that your teacher's policy is designed to handle only "ordinary" episodes of missing an exam—as in Christy's and Jennifer's cases. Equity lets your professor say that the rule simply doesn't cover Rehan's special circum-stances. Equity allows a solution to be devised that will fit. Equity doesn't require identical treatment; it requires that people be treated approp-riately to the circumstances.

So what does this case look like from the perspective of the "ethic of care"? Remembering that the central moral command of the ethic of care is to "discern and alleviate the 'real and recognizable trouble' of this world," we can first appreciate that by helping Mark, Rehan was attend-ing to a higher responsibility than to fulfill his obligations to be in class. It then wouldn't seem right to punish him for doing what he had a moral responsibility to do. Also, considering how serious this matter is and how deeply it's affecting Rehan, he's not going to be getting any practical advantage from having more time to prepare for the exam. When we incorporate the principle of equity, which lets us mold our response to the situation, we can see that the appropriate thing to do is to let Rehan take the make-up without any penalty, but enforcing the announced policy for Chris and Jenny.

Two Ethical Voices

If Gilligan is right, this means that there are fundamental differ-ences in the way people work through moral dilemmas from start to finish. These differences would encompass: what counts as an ethical issue in the first place; how serious it actually is; how to resolve it; and how to evaluate one's final decision. As Gilligan puts it, there are two moral "voices." One emphasizes equality, justice, and rights; the other speaks of care, responsibility, and human connections.

The obvious question to ask is whether one of these two ethics is better than the other. Gilligan argues, however, that they are actually complementary—that both of them should be a part of our moral reasoning. Accordingly, she encourages "justice" people to make the effort to see what a care perspective would tell them about a moral dilemma, and vice versa. We have, then, two perspectives that are simply different.

Ultimately, Gilligan claims that most people have both of these "voices," so to call these "male" and "female" approaches to moral reasoning is somewhat misleading. Nonetheless, most people use the approach or "moral style" which is characteristic of their sex. In addition, the question of the source of this difference is at this point irrelevant, that is, whether it is simply socialization into traditional sex roles, the result of the greater use by women of the right hemisphere of their brain, or some other reason. The point of this discussion is simply to let you know that there are these different approaches. By understanding them better, you can accept, understand, and work more effectively with the people you find using them.

Actually, it seems to me that there is a rough parallel between these two ethics and the two approaches I talked about earlier. In many ways, the ethic of care's concern with preventing harm and its focus on the context in which actions take place is like a results-oriented approach. In the same way, the ethic of justice's concern with equal respect for people's rights is similar to an act-oriented approach. Nonetheless, there are dimensions of the difference Gilligan talks about that are not covered by reducing it to this. So try to consider this on its own merits.

As interesting as the differences are between Kohlberg and Gilligan, they shouldn't obscure that the two psychologists agree there is such a thing as moral development and that it is grounded in the human personality. While the two of them might disagree about how they evaluate certain types of moral reasoning, they are both committed to the idea that certain ways of thinking about and resolving ethical dilemmas are mature and well developed and others come up short. And as with Maslow, you have to remember that these people have spent years doing empirical research on this issue. Idle speculation it isn't.

CONCLUSION

For all the discussion, this chapter contains only two rather simple and straightforward claims—that ethical behavior is one of the traits of the mature, strong, healthy, and fully developed human personality; and that unethical behavior ultimately has a negative effect on us. We've looked at dimensions of these theses through a whole range of sources—Greek philosophy, medieval Christian thought, modern science fiction, and contemporary psychology—and while there are important differences among them, they all back up the heart of these ideas.

DISCUSSION QUESTIONS

1. What's your reaction to the two main claims of this chapter?
   Ethical behavior is one of the traits of the mature, strong, healthy, and fully developed human personality;
   Unethical behavior ultimately has a negative effect on us.

2. Have you found it true in your own life that once you started doing something you used to think is wrong (cheating, lying, stealing), it got easier and you did it more often? Or did you find the exact opposite—that you did it once and were so upset with yourself that you stopped? If the latter is the case, does that prove Socrates wrong?

3. To some extent, what people like Socrates and Maslow claim about morality and the healthy, fully developed personality doesn't fit with some basic ideas in our society. We're told that aggressively competing and trying to advance our own interests is a sign of strength. Someone "who doesn't have the stomach to play hard ball" is seen as a wimp. What's your reaction to this?

4. Consider the following example. You work at a record store. On Monday night your boss has to leave early and asks you to lock up for her. At closing time you put everything away, lock the back door, and look around to make sure everything's O.K. You know there's a window in the back room but you don't check it because nobody ever opens it. In the morning you come in and find out that someone came in through the window and made off with half of the store's inventory. You remember that you never checked the window. You have two options: (a) tell your boss the truth and see what happens; (b) swear to her that you locked the window and convince her that the thieves must have found some other way to get in (your boss trusts you and the circumstances of the theft are such that you could probably get away with it). Which of these is the stronger thing to do? Telling the truth may require honesty and a willingness to accept some unpleasant consequences, but if you do that you aren't looking after your own interests very well. Besides, insurance will cover the loss and you figure you've learned your lesson about checking

every detail, no matter how small. On the other hand, telling the story will take a little imagination and discipline. You know that you're basically a good worker but that your boss may feel compelled to fire you no matter what. If you lie (you tell yourself), you're showing that you know how to protect yourself in the "real" world.

5. Do you see any differences in how men and women identify and resolve ethical dilemmas?

chapter 6

Cheating: An Ethical Dilemma

So far, we've discussed what ethics is, what a standard of human happiness could look like, how you measure the consequences of an action, how you evaluate the action itself, and why we should concern ourselves with acting ethically. This chapter will show you how these ideas can work in real life. Ordinary ethical dilemmas don't come neatly prepared for analysis. How do you know when something in your life is an ethical problem? How do you balance off what you get by looking at the consequences on one hand, and the actions on the other? (People like Mill and Kant would see a results-oriented approach and an action-oriented approach being opposed to one another, but I believe that to get a full picture you have to use both.) And is giving in to the ordinary temptations we face daily—which are much less dramatic than the kinds of situations Socrates or Luke Skywalker were in—really going to hurt us?

You might understand this better with an extended example of how it can be used in real life ethical dilemmas. I'm going to choose a case of the sort that you no doubt face at this point in your life. But as should be obvious by now, you can use the analytical skills I've been introducing you to on any moral dilemmas you confront in life.

CHEATING—RIGHT OR WRONG?

An ethical dilemma that you unquestionably face in college is whether or not to cheat. This can include a whole range of things: sneaking a look at someone else's exam, letting someone copy your answers, using homework or papers from a fraternity's file, having a friend do assignments for you, buying or even stealing a term paper to turn in under your own name.

Cheating is pretty common. And yet there isn't a college or university in this land that doesn't have rules and policies against it. This could mean that lots of students think there's nothing (or at least not very much) wrong with it. Are they right? How does cheating measure up from an ethical standpoint? Is it right or wrong?

To do this right, we need a specific example. We could look at cheating in general, but there's little point to that. After all, "cheating in general" doesn't exist in the world you and I live in. Cheating by specific people in particular situations does. We should start, then, with all of the relevant facts in the open. By the way, this is, as it were, Rule 1 in an ethical analysis—know as many facts about the specific case as you can.

Consider this example. You and your good friend Diane take a lot of the same courses, but you have different strengths. She's really good in math, science, and computers; you're better in philosophy, history, and languages. You care a good deal about each other and really want one another to do well in life. You study together and try to help each other in your respective weak areas. In fact, every now and then you'll improve one of Diane's papers by substantially rewriting it. In return, you copy her lab reports from biology and turn in the programs she wrote when she took the computer course. Whenever you take exams, the two of you position yourselves so that the one who's weaker in the subject can see the other's answers. It's a good arrangement. The two of you are getting better grades than you would by just working on your own. On one hand, this seems like a really positive thing to be doing—two friends helping each other. But on the other hand, the two of you are cheating like mad. Isn't there something unethical about all of this?

WHY IS THIS AN ETHICAL ISSUE?

Let's begin by asking why this is an ethical issue. Recall from Chapter 2 that ethics' primary function is to evaluate an action against a very basic standard of human happiness, well-being or satisfaction with life. Accordingly, we have an ethical issue on our hands whenever any of the things we need for such a sense of well-being is involved. And since these needs fall into two general categories—specific material conditions and ways of being treated—we only have to look to see if either one is on the line. If so, then we're entitled to haul out our ethical yardstick and see how the situation measures up.

What about the case at hand? There are a variety of reasons why this is an ethical issue. It looks like there's deception going on (you're claiming someone else's work as your own) which also involves you in manipulating someone (your professor) and breaking an agreement (about how you'll act). This creates inequality between you and students who aren't getting the same kind of help (the conditions under which you're receiving grades are now different). Your actions are helping and/or hindering yourselves and other students in getting what you want in life (grades, a diploma, a career). Each of these can have an important effect on the search for a satisfying or happy human life, and that's all we need to make the situation a candidate for ethical analysis. Between questions about the intrinsic merit of what you're doing and the potential benefit or harm to you and others, there's enough in this case to elicit careful scrutiny.

Identifying the ethical issues involved doesn't mean we've made any judgment about what's going on. Evaluating the case is our next step. It may turn out that the cheating is justifiable. (We may be mistaken about our initial reading of the situation. Closer examination may convince us that the deception, inequality, and harm aren't all that serious or are more than made up for by the good that's produced.) On the other hand, we may decide that it's wrong. (We might conclude that the harm outweighs the good or that the actions are just wrong in themselves.) But at least we see that some appraisal of the case is needed.

ANALYZING THE ACTIONS INVOLVED

Although an act-oriented (deontological) approach to ethics is harder to explain than a results-oriented (teleological) one, it's easier in an actual ethical analysis to look at the actions first. As I said in Chapter 4, your focus is much narrower when you're looking just at the actions. The main facets of this case that make it an ethical one are deception, manipulation, breaking an agreement, conflicting responsibilities, and inequality.

Deception

The *deception* involved is a critical part of this case. You and Diane are misrepresenting to your teachers that your work is your own, and this seriously violates the integrity of the educational process. The "rules of the game" are well known and explicitly stated in the regulations of every college and university. One job of educational institutions is to evaluate their students' intellectual abilities. When I give Diane a B in my ethics course, I'm saying, "I hereby certify that I have examined Diane's work and found that she has an above average ability in analyzing ethical issues and presenting arguments in support of her positions." But for that statement to mean what it says, I have to be speaking about Diane's work, not your work handed in under Diane's name. If it's your work, then Diane is lying to me. So the first problem here is that truth is a casualty in the process.

Manipulation

But keep in mind why you and Diane are lying about whose work it is. If Diane hands in a paper to me that you actually wrote (or at least significantly improved), you and she are trying to mislead me in my evaluation of her work. That is, you're trying to *manipulate* me so that I give her a higher grade than she deserves. You're trying to deceive me because you know this is something I'd never condone. You're asking me to compromise myself as a professional and lie in my evaluation of your work. And since I won't agree to it, you're trying to trick me into it. So the second ethical problem here is that you're using me for your own ends. This, of course, should bring to mind Kant's standard that our actions should treat one another as "ends in themselves" and not only as "means."

Breaking an Agreement

Next, notice that there's an issue here of keeping your word. The point to see is that by participating in courses and a program of study, you agree to abide by the policies set down by the institution. It's like entering into a contract or making a promise. And the most fundamental "term of the agreement," as it were, is that the work you present for evaluation will be your own. No matter whether you or anyone else is helped or hurt by the deception, when you hand in Diane's work as yours or when she copies your answer on an exam, you're *breaking an agreement* that you freely entered. From an ethical standpoint, that's a serious matter.

(By the way, it doesn't matter than you haven't signed a statement or formally pledged your agreement. You can't be on a college campus long and not understand what's expected of you. As long as you play the game, the rest of the players assume that you're going to abide by the rules. It's the same with the law. If you act as though you have an agreement with someone, a court will regard you as having a contract with that person. It doesn't matter that there's no formal document. This is called a "tacit" [unspoken] or "implied" contract.)

Actually, breaking the agreement to be honest in your work is more than just a serious matter. There are many regulations that you implicitly agree to follow when you go to college, but this is one of the most important. The agreement to be judged on your own work is what makes it possible for schools to evaluate and certify students. Without that agreement you wouldn't have grades or degrees.

Now you may think that grades and degrees are meaningless. However, evaluating and certifying students is currently the second most important activity of colleges and universities—helping people learn is the most important. So despite what you think about grades, one of the first provisions in the implied agreement with your college or university is about academic honesty. Breaking your agreement on something this important to the enterprise is an extremely serious offense. The only thing worse would be to disrupt classes or try to control what ideas get discussed in class or in public lectures.

The issue of breaking an agreement is very close to Kant's example of making a "false promise." So the discussion about that point from Chapter 4 is also relevant here. It should be clear that when you break your agreement, your promise and your deeds are inconsistent and you're using your teacher for your own ends. None of this measures up very well against an ethical yardstick.

Conflicting Responsibilities

Perhaps you and Diane fully understand that you're breaking your word, but still think it's justifiable. Maybe you feel that you have conflicting responsibilities.

"In one way," you say, "I have an obligation to keep my agreement. But I also have a responsibility to help my friend. That's what it means to be friends—to help one another, to be loyal. Surely, if we're looking at actions themselves, 'helping a friend' is at least as good as 'keeping an agreement.' And in my opinion, it's better. It's a higher responsibility. 'Keeping an agreement' is abstract, rational and cold. 'Helping a friend' is humane, generous, and compassionate. I think it's closer to 'promoting human good,' which is, after all, what ethics is supposed to be all about."

Good point. On the surface you paint a picture of *conflicting responsibilities* between which you must choose—something that's very common in real life. If you make a date to go to Saturday's game with Barbara and then remember that you'd already asked Grace, you've got conflicting obligations. How do you resolve it? Well, looking to see if one clearly takes priority is the best way to approach this. (And by "taking priority" I mean ethically, not whether you'd rather go with Barbara because she drives a Ferrari.) This is what you did in saying that "helping a friend" is more important than "keeping an agreement." This is also what

Chapter 5 discussed about equity—that Rehan's obligation to his troubled friend Mark took priority over his responsibility to be in class for an exam.

But is your resolution of the problem of conflicting responsibilities persuasive? Not to me. Because you're ignoring the fact that you already have an agreement with your school that prohibits precisely the kind of help you and Diane are giving each other. And that means that the obligations you feel aren't simply conflicting but *mutually exclusive.* You can usually find a compromise between obligations which conflict (Rehan can take the exam later); not if they're mutually exclusive. To meet one you must give up the other. To fulfill your agreement with the school, you and Diane may not help each other if it involves misrepresenting your work. On the other hand, if you feel that there should be no limits to the obligations between friends, you can't in good faith remain in college.

Inequality

We've talked about deception, manipulation, and breaking your agreement. The other questionable facet of what you and Diane are doing is the *inequality* your actions are creating. As a result of your pact with Diane, the conditions under which you and students who don't cheat are being judged are now different. It would be the same as if you were running a five-mile race and you have a friend run miles three and four for you while all the other runners keep going and you rest on the sidelines for a big finish. An equal and fair competition this isn't.

(The inequality is in one sense a consequence of breaking your agreement. In another sense it's as much a part of your action as not intending to pay is a part of a false promise. You're manipulating the situation in a way that allows your misrepresentations to get you and Diane different treatment. This shows that in real cases, actions and consequences may become hard to distinguish.)

In a way this goes back to keeping your promise, because your agreement would also contain the idea that you're willing to be evaluated on an equal footing with other students. The assumption is that in order for everyone to be judged fairly, they have to be judged under equal conditions. This reflects the basic idea that all humans are equal and that none are entitled to special treatment unless some special conditions exist. In a free society such as ours, violating a principle of human equality is no small matter. Few things are more essential for a basic sense of dignity than respecting the equality of our brothers and sisters. I can't really think of how you and Diane could argue that your situation was so special as to set aside a principle of such fundamental human importance as equality.

Universalizing Your Maxims

In Chapter 4 I explained a couple of Kant's formulations of the moral law (categorical imperative). One talked about treating people as "ends in themselves"; the other about being able to will the maxims of your actions as a universal law. Between the two of them Kant gave us ways of judging how our actions measure up to standards of human autonomy and rationality. By talking about manipulation and equality above, we've effectively covered Kant's concern about respecting people's dignity. So we should see how the rest of what he says adds to our analysis.

Asking whether you're "using" someone for your own ends is easy to understand. Everybody knows what being manipulated means. Asking whether you can "universalize the maxims of your action" is another story. As we saw from Kant's explanation, however, the way to check this is to ask what the world would look like if everybody acted according to the general principle your action is based on. So what's the maxim that governs what you and Diane are doing? Let's try something like: "Whenever I judge it to be to my advantage, I will use deception and misrepresentation. I will do so despite a clear pledge (even if implicit) to the contrary and despite the fact that this will put others at a disadvantage."

What would a world based on that maxim be like? Pretty nasty. First, as with Kant's example of the false promise, the notion of a pledge or agreement wouldn't even exist. If everyone knows that no one's going to keep agreements if it's not in their interest, no one would make agreements in the first place. Second, distrust and the aggressive pursuit of self-interest would be rife. And since people would still have to work together and yet want to be protected from one another's scheming, instruments of coercion would take the place of promises. How does such a world measure up against notions of human dignity, equality, and honesty? Not very well.

The "Bottom Line" on Actions

So you've got a bunch of actions here that don't seem to pass "philosophical muster"—deception, manipulation, agreement breaking, and inequality. About the only thing that seems positive is your sense of loyalty and obligation to help your friend. But even so, we saw that it was already precluded by your agreement with your school.

So far, cheating isn't faring very well. Let's take a look at the consequences, then, and see what that adds to the analysis.

CONSEQUENCES

When we analyze the consequences, we get to look at more of the real life specifics of the case. So our basic question is: Does any real harm come from what you and Diane are doing? Your first reaction will probably be "no."

No Harm?

"What we're doing isn't like stealing," you might say. "We aren't taking something that belongs to someone else. Even if you copy someone's answer on an exam without their knowing it, you're not taking anything away from them. They don't lose anything. But even so, we're not doing that. We're giving each other something of our own."

Diane might add, "And no one's getting hurt by what we're doing. We aren't doing anything violent in any way. We aren't interfering with what anyone else wants to do. We are just trying to help each other out. If other people want to do that too, that's fine with us. There's no coercion or manipulation involved here."

Picking up on the idea of "helping each other," you explain, "Look, if anything, what we're doing results only in good, not harm. Nobody's getting hurt and the two of us are ending up ahead in the game. We help each other get better grades in our weak subjects. I learn what I can about computer programming, for instance, and then I use Diane's assignments from last semester. Without them I'd get a C in the course. But I don't want Cs; I want Bs. With Bs I'll graduate with a higher average and stand a better chance of getting into graduate school or getting the kind of job I want. Diane wants to go to medical school, and you know how important averages are for that. But she's not as good as I am with writing and ideas. So she does what she can and then I give her a boost. What difference is it going to make to Diane's patients if she really understands Thomas More's *Utopia?* But it could make a big difference in her getting into a good medical school if she can ace her philosophy course. See, the bottom line is all positive."

Short-Term Harm

So far it looks like your mutual assistance pact isn't doing anybody any harm, but is it that simple? First of all, what if your professor grades on a curve? In that case, when you get a higher grade than you deserve, someone else is probably getting a lower grade than they would if you didn't have Diane's help. And it looks like there's an element of stealing there. You're taking away from somebody else a grade that is rightfully theirs. So if the grades are curved, someone is getting hurt. And they're being hurt now (lowered grade) and perhaps also in the future (if their lowered average causes them to lose out on something).

But what if your teacher doesn't curve grades? Considering what we were just talking about, does that mean that no one's being harmed? Well, it's probably true now that no one in your class is being hurt. Your professor is just giving out more As or Bs than she would otherwise. No one's being hurt in the short run.

Is there anyone else who might be unhappy in the short run? Well, if your instructors suspect what you're up to, they're going to start feeling troubled. The same can be said for other students who know and disapprove. And don't overlook that as long as you and Diane are cheating, you're going to be feeling some anxiety. You've got to worry about being caught and what the consequences will be. Maybe this isn't harm, but it's not pleasure either.

Not Harm But Self-Defense

Now at this point you might say,

"If harm's such a big issue, you've got to see it both ways. Maybe somebody loses out on a grade. But all we're doing is keeping ourselves from getting harmed. Be realistic. Places in medical school, jobs, and promotions aren't handed out simply according to an objective evaluation of grades or abilities. First, lots of other people cheat, and some do stuff a whole lot worse than what Diane and I are doing—like sabotaging laboratory experiments, stealing books or articles from the library that the rest of the class needs. We aren't trying to hurt anybody else. We're just trying to keep from getting hurt ourselves.

"Second, jobs and seats in medical school are often given out for what we think are the wrong reasons—who you know in the company, whether you're good looking, whether your father's given his alma mater some big bucks over the years, the university's desire to have a class that's mixed in terms of geography, race, and sex. Trying to get an edge with our grades is just our way of trying to keep even in the game. We're just trying to offset some of the unfairness that we know is out there.

"In fact, this should even help other people. Diane and I are honest, responsible, and hard working. If a little cheating will give me an edge over someone who may not do a job as well as I will (and who maybe got where he is through connections), then my company's going to benefit too. We get helped. Other people get helped."

This isn't a bad piece of reasoning. It's based on a realistic appraisal of a complex situation, and it takes a look at the long term. If you know you're involved in an unfair competition, isn't being unfair yourself the only protection against unfair treatment? Maybe so, in the short run. But let's look at the long haul more closely. What are the consequences over time of your acting this way?

Long Term—Others

There are two ways to approach this question: the long-term effects of your actions on others and the consequences on yourself. From what you just said, there are some positive consequences worth mentioning. Maybe your success will be at the expense of someone who wouldn't do as good a job as you. And perhaps when you get into a position of power or responsibility, you can do something to try to make things fairer for others.

But does that also mean that no one will be harmed in the future? I don't think so. After all, if your calculation is right that a boosted average may get you a place in graduate school or a job that you wouldn't have gotten, you're assuming that it will let you beat out someone else for that slot. If Diane gets accepted at Harvard Medical School, someone else is being rejected because of that. In fact, the whole aim of helping each other is so that you'll do better later in life—that is, do better than other people. By getting higher grades, you're trying to block someone else's attempt to get what he or she wants. Trying to interfere with someone else's life in a way that's outside the "rules of the game" strikes me as a pretty aggressive enterprise. So the premise that has you doing all of this in the first place ("higher grades help in life") shows that the only reason you're cheating is to hurt somebody else eventually. Of course, you'll probably never have to face your victims—which makes this whole process easier—but that doesn't mean they don't exist and that their pain isn't real.

However, the main, long-term, negative consequences are that you're reinforcing the very unfairness you've just been complaining about. You're cheating only out of self-defense. You see other people doing it, and so you do it as well. Maybe this keeps you even, but it probably also encourages other people to do the same as you and Diane. If other people's cheating got you to do it, why won't yours help others along the same path? Further-more, it's possible that when you run into unfair situations in the future, you'll again feel that it's O.K. to be a little unscrupulous yourself—just to protect yourself from harm again in an unfair world. But, of course, every time you act that way, you do your part in keeping it unfair. And you're giving other people good reason to believe that if they want a fair shake, their cheating is necessary to protect themselves from people like you. This is also a consequence that you'll probably never see, but that doesn't mean it isn't real.

Also, remember what Mill did when he looked at the very long-term effects of lying. In this case, you're performing a bunch of questionable actions—deception, manipulation, agreement breaking, creating a situa-tion that's unfair to other students, and taking benefits away from other people. Your actions will to some extent break down trust between people and will encourage other people to act like you in self-defense. Over the long haul, this is only going to harm the society you live in.

Of course, in the current situation, cheating may effectively protect your own short-term interests. But at the same time, you can't avoid the fact that over the longer haul your cheating is keeping the game unfair and making things worse for other people. I'm not saying that if you don't cheat, the game will become fair overnight. However, not cheating is the only thing that will make any difference in the long term.

Long Term—You

And as long as we're talking about long-term consequences, what about the effect on you and Diane as individuals? The most obvious positive consequences are that the two of you may end up better off in exactly the way you've planned because of the cheating—better grades and a better future.

But is there a down side as well? Not surprisingly. First, let's consider the possibility that you get caught. (You may not think the risk of being caught is much, but a thorough analysis requires that you consider all the consequences.) Depending on the university's penalties and your personal situation, this could range from failing the course to expulsion, and from simple embarrassment with your friends to big trouble with your parents, and to difficulty later on in life because this is on your record.

However, even if you get away with it, there are still negative conse-quences. The main point to see on this is that we all act in patterns. We're certainly capable of acting in a way that doesn't fit our standard patterns, but that's more the exception. As a rule, if we do something and it works for us, we're probably going to do it again. (Behavioral psychologists call this positive reinforcement.) If you and Diane are succeeding in your cheating, the odds are you'll continue—and that you'll continue after you graduate. If this has worked for you at school, why stop there? Why not do the same on the job, if you can? All you need is enough justification. Maybe you feel you've been passed over too often for a promotion, so you tell your boss that the suggestion somebody else made was really yours or you exaggerate the shortcomings of a co-worker. Perhaps Diane thinks that health insurance doesn't pay enough, so she puts in a few phony claims. But if you've succeeded in the past and you think you've got enough reason to do it again, you will.

After all, if successful cheating makes it more likely that you'll do it in the future, it's probably also making you think there's less wrong with it. Once you break down your initial resistance, rationalizations are easy to find. I'm not going to say that what you and Diane are doing is going to take you from cheating in college to lying on job applications to cheating on your spouse to callous manipulation of your employees or embezzlement. (That would be a logical fallacy we call the "slippery slope." One step in the wrong direction and—BAM!—you're over the edge.) But it is realistic to suggest that over the long haul you'll do or tolerate more dishonesty than you would have if you hadn't adopted this pattern of acting. You certainly won't use your future position of responsibility to make the game fair for others, because by that time you'll have decided that this is just "the way it is." You'll deal with your friends and associates from this perspective. And you'll teach it to your children. You will no longer be the honest person just doing a few dishonest things to protect yourself. In the future you'll *be* dishonest. *How* dishonest will depend on how deep you've gotten yourself. But that's just a matter of degree. You'll have crossed the line.

Bentham and Mill

I tried to go through the consequences in this case in a commonsense fashion without reference to Bentham and Mill, but I think it'd be useful to see if Bentham's and Mill's ideas have anything to add.

You'll remember that Bentham gave us the hedonistic calculus, but there are so many problems with this system that there's no reason to go through as Bentham would suggest. However, it's worth taking a quick look at the different categories he mentions. In fact, let's simply cover Mill's ideas by adding an eighth category—quality—to Bentham's seven.

Intensity Presuming that the cheating really pays off for you and Diane later in life, the pleasure should be fairly intense. There's no disputing that success feels good. However, I think the unhappiness that people will feel from all of this would be more intense. Similarly, suspecting or finding out that you've been deceived and used by someone feels really rotten.

Duration Your pleasure will probably last longer than other people's pains, if you're able to build on your successes. Assuming that your cheating won't do irrevocable harm to someone, he or she ought to be able to get over it.

Certainty Realistically, we can't say just how likely it is that the cheating will pay off the way you want. Maybe it will, but maybe it won't make as big a difference as you think. Getting hired or admitted to graduate school depends on a lot more than your college transcript. You and Diane might end up with the same jobs or schools that you would have if you didn't cheat. Of course, that also means that we don't know the certainty of your hurting people by displacing them from jobs they would have gotten. However, the pain felt by students who don't like what you're doing and by faculty who may only suspect it is certain. Even entertaining the possibility that a student is cheating makes most teachers very angry.

Propinquity Your pleasure will begin as soon as you start getting higher grades. Any unhappiness will wait at least until you were discovered. Major unhappiness in someone else's life might not be for years.

Fecundity The cheating could really produce big dividends for the two of you—good grades, professional success, money, reputation.

Purity You aren't going to escape without some unhappiness. There's the anxiety connected with pulling some of this off (like cheating on an in-class exam) and the overall fear of being caught, which will last as long as your scheme does. If you've got any conscience, you'll feel at least some guilt. And, as we've seen, this could produce major unhappiness in other people's lives.

Extent The benefits of cheating will in the short term go primarily to you and Diane. In the longer term other people could get pleasure out of it too. Your friends and families—from your good marks and later success; your clients, companies or patients—from your performance on the job. The extent of the harm will depend on how well you cheat. If you do it really well, you could beat out many people for a variety of things (grades, jobs, promotions, money) in the course of your life. You could also contribute to the decision of a lot of people to be deceitful. The number of people harmed indirectly could then be sizable. To offset this, you and Diane would have to do an awful lot of good for other people throughout your lives.

Quality This is the kicker. Success achieved through dishonesty would rate very low in Mill's mind. You're experiencing material pleasures achieved through selfishness, callous disregard for others, deceit, manipulation, and unfairness. The quality of the corresponding pain of your victims, then, would be high.

Consequences—The "Bottom Line"

Our examination of the consequences gives us a mixed bag—good and harm for both you and others. My own judgment is that the harm outweighs the good, especially when we factor in quality and the very long-term results. But, of course, since we're talking about judgment rather than any kind of empirical measure, that's open to debate.

SUMMARY

So this is what an extended ethical analysis looks like. In this case, we see that the actions involved are by and large questionable and that they produce a combination of good and harm. The benefits are personal, material, and professional success for you and Diane. The good that will come from this will probably be somewhat limited, although this depends on what you do with your lives. However, the harm seems to be worse than the good produced. And over the long haul it could directly or indirectly worsen the lives of a large number of people.

A FINAL WORD

So now you've been introduced to the basics of philosophical ethics. You probably don't feel as though your life has taken a dramatic turn because of what you've learned. But if you've followed me throughout this handbook, you should know what goes on in an ethical analysis, be able to do it yourself, and understand why many of us think philosophical ethics is useful and important. In concluding, then, I want to commend you for your hard work. I hope you feel the effort was worth it, and that I've helped make a difference in how you see things.

DISCUSSION QUESTIONS

1. What's your reaction to this analysis of the cheating case? Where is it accurate? Where is it off target? Do you think there's anything *wrong* going on in the case described? Explain your thinking.

2. When you face an everyday ethical dilemma you obviously aren't going to subject it to a full-scale ethical analysis. However, what will you do? Will you use anything that you've learned in this book? (Be honest!)

3. Analyze the following cases. Decide whether you think anything *wrong* is going on. What's your judgment based on?

    a. In the course of a conversation with your father about a news story, he tells you that he'd never want "heroic measures" used to save him if he were ill or in an accident. (Your mother and two younger brothers aren't home at the time.) A couple of years later he's hurt badly in a car crash and only if heroic measures are taken does he stand a chance. Because you're deeply attached to your father, you tell your mother that he once told you that in a situation like this he'd want absolutely everything possible done to save him.

    b. A group of people opposed to abortion set up a "Pregnancy Problem Center." Their aim is to make young women think that it's an abortion clinic. They use deliberately vague advertisements and evasive answers over the telephone. The goal is to have women come to their center so that they can try to talk them out of having an abortion. Their critics charge them with "deception."

    c. You've been married for a few years and you have a child. You're off on a business trip on the other side of the country. You've never been unfaithful to your spouse before, but you meet this really attractive person at your hotel. The two of you end up in bed together. You're sure this is only going to be a "one night stand" and that your spouse will never find out.

ADDITIONAL READINGS

If you're interested in learning more about ethics, there are a number of good introductory books that go into detail and are more technical than this one. For starters you can look at William K. Frankena, *Ethics* (Englewood Cliffs, N.J.: Prentice-Hall, 1973); Richard L. Purtill, *Thinking*

About Ethics (Englewood Cliffs, N.J.: Prentice-Hall, 1976); James Rachels, *The Elements of Moral Philosophy* (New York: Random House, 1986); and Robert C. Solomon, *Ethics: A Brief Introduction* (New York: McGraw Hill, 1984). You can also find good articles and bibliographies on a variety of topics connected with ethics in *The Encyclopedia of Philosophy* (New York: Macmillan, 1967).

A good sampler of different philosophers writing on ethics is A. I. Melden, *Ethical Theories* (Englewood Cliffs, N.J.: Prentice-Hall, 1967).

If you want to learn more about the ideas of the writers I mentioned in the course of discussion, read: *The Trial and Death of Socrates*, translated by G. M. A. Grube (Indianapolis, Indiana: Hackett, 1975); John Stuart Mill, *Utilitarianism* (Indianapolis, Indiana: Bobbs-Merrill, 1957); Immanuel Kant, *Grounding for the Metaphysics of Morals* (Indianapolis, Indiana: Hackett, 1981); Saint Augustine, *On Free Choice of the Will* (Indianapolis, Indiana: Bobbs-Merrill, 1964); A. H. Maslow, *The Farther Reaches of Human Nature* (New York: Penguin, 1971); Lawrence Kohlberg, *The Philosophy of Moral Development* (San Francisco: Harper and Row, 1981); and Carol Gilligan, *In A Different Voice* (Cambridge, Massachusetts: Harvard, 1982).

Glossary

Categorical imperative—According to Kant, a moral principle against which we can measure our actions; a command (imperative) that holds without qualification (categorically).

Consequence—Result; the amount or type of human good or harm produced by an action. A teleological (results-oriented) approach to ethics focuses exclusively on consequences.

Conventional moral reasoning—According to Kohlberg, a stage in which the moral standard is determined by one's family or society.

Deontological—An ethical approach which evaluates actions according to their intrinsic value, without reference to their results; act-oriented; from *deontos*, the Greek word for "duty."

Empiricism—An intellectual approach which emphasizes the importance of studying the physical world. Modern science is "empirical" science.

Ethical yardstick—A standard of human good against which we can gauge the moral worth of actions.

Ethic of care—According to Gilligan, morality of responsibility; an ethical approach based on a responsibility to help others and minimize harm; more contextual than objective and impartial; described in Gilligan's research.

Ethic of justice—According to Gilligan, morality of rights; an ethical approach based on principles of treating people equally and fairly;

more objective and impartial than contextual; described in Kohlberg's research.

Ethics—Moral philosophy; a branch of philosophy dating back 2,000 years to Socrates, which studies right and wrong and advances theories about how to determine the morality of actions.

Equality—A principle which maintains that similar cases should be treated the same.

Equity—A principle which maintains that similar cases can be treated differently, depending on the circumstances.

Hedonistic calculus—Bentham's system for measuring the pleasure or pain that an action produces, based on seven elements (intensity, duration, certainty, propinquity, fecundity, purity, and extent).

Human happiness, human good, human well-being—Different ways of referring to the ultimate standard used in philosophical ethics; a state of affairs brought about by our distinctly human needs being met. Ethics' overall aim is simply to evaluate how much an action fosters human good.

Maxim—According to Kant, the principle governing an action; similar to a policy statement.

Moral development theory—The branch of contemporary psychology that examines how humans think about ethical issues.

Moral vision—The ability to see the ethical character of an action and its consequences.

Morality of responsibility—See Ethic of care.

Morality of justice—See Ethic of justice.

Morals—Same as ethics.

Philosophical ethics—An approach to evaluating how right or wrong actions are that depends on a strictly rational approach and secular standards.

Postconventional ethics—According to Kohlberg, a stage in which reasoning about the morality of actions is based on universal ethical principles.

Preconventional ethics—According to Kohlberg, a stage in which reasoning about the morality of actions is based on punishment, reward, and authority.

Reason—The mind, the intellect; mental operations governed by the rules of logic.

Result—See Consequence.

Standard—A basis against which to judge things.

Strength of will—The power to act ethically in the face of temptations to the contrary.

Teleological—An ethical approach which evaluates actions according to their consequences or how much good or harm results; results-oriented; from *telos,* the Greek word for "end."

Utilitarianism—A philosophical approach fashioned by Bentham and Mill which evaluates actions or policies according to how useful they are, that is, how much they improve life.

Index